The After-50 Cookbook

The After-50 Cookbook

A Treasury of Creative Recipes for 1 or 2, Retired People, or Those on Special Diets

BY

DONNA HAMILTON

THE SWALLOW PRESS INC.
CHICAGO

First Edition
    First Printing   November 1974
    Second Printing   January 1975

Published by
The Swallow Press Incorporated
1139 South Wabash Avenue
Chicago, Illinois 60605

ISBN (clothbound edition) 0-8040-0667-9
LIBRARY OF CONGRESS CATALOG CARD NUMBER 74-16551

Dedication

Mentors are perhaps the greatest and most golden influence in life. For me, the first was Betty Liljestrom; then came Mae Boettcher, soon followed by Helen Johnson and Marian Talmadge.

To them with thanks for their love, friendship, counseling and guidance this book is gratefully dedicated.

DMH

Contents

Introduction

A cookbook for which there is a real need and specific purpose is indeed a pleasure to write. It develops with a natural ease, and soon it becomes apparent that the only limitation is space itself.

The research and recipe-testing for this collection brought forth, in flavorful abundance, new ways for vitality and versatility in cooking for one or two people. Even the dictates of the five most common, physician-prescribed diets turn out to have more emotional implication than restrictive application.

There are many reliable new products in the supermarkets that meet the requirements for those on low-sodium, low-cholesterol, sugar-restricted, low-calorie, and low-ruffage diets. If there isn't a helpful product, there is a cooking method or a savory and satisfying solution such as the use of herbs, spirits . . . and ingenuity.

If you are looking on the near, or the far, side of fifty — on a diet on not — this cookbook of kitchen-tested recipes is written for you.

It includes:

Recipes designed to serve one or two people, or to yield small batches of cookies, petite pies, mini-cakes, and breads.

Recipes formulated for cooking or baking in small-size pans or baking dishes and in kitchens with limited cabinet and freezer space.

Recipes that offer a comfortable choice for less adventuresome cooks, a challenge for others, and a good cross-section of all-time favorites and new innovations.

Recipes that will be useful for more than one occasion as well as more than one diet with broad freedom in ingredient options and alternatives. Primary consideration has been given to leaving the "left" out of leftovers and giving them the rank of "firstovers."

Recipes built with inherent economy by the use of budget-conscious ingredients without shortchanging the end result.

Recipes that encourage the cook to exercise personal preference in using fresh, frozen, or canned products.

Pre-recipe comments that give helpful hints for making optimum use of a recipe; alert the cook to such pertinent facts as packaged sauce, soup, and other mixes containing salt and sugar that are off-limits for those on restricted diets, or pointing out special virtues of a recipe for freezing and the like.

Instructions that are simple, explicit and uncluttered with superfluous procedures such as flour sifting or easily eliminated pan washing.

THE AFTER-50 COOKBOOK is meant to be a versatile collection to meet most personal food preferences or diets, all occasions, what is on the pantry shelf or in the pocket book . . . and the weather, if need be. Cooking after-fifty is not broiled steak or chops, leftovers and small cans of vegetables. It is a pleasing, rewarding experience filled with selective, varied, and ofttimes gourmet meals. Enter in and enjoy.

DONNA HAMILTON
Denver, Colorado
June, 1974

Appetizers

Braunschweiger or Liverwurst Spread

Rye-flavored crackers, toast-rounds, and flat breads are the partymates for this paté. Can be made well in advance and keeps well. Divide recipe in half if smaller amount is desired.

8 ounces braunschweiger or liverwurst

3 tablespoons mayonnaise or diet mayonnaise

2 tablespoons sour cream or sour cream substitute

¼ teaspoon dried or 2 teaspoons fresh, chopped parsley

½ teaspoon instant minced or 1 teaspoon minced onion

Few drops Tabasco

¼ teaspoon pepper or lemon pepper

2 tablespoons brandy or cognac (optional)

2 hard-cooked eggs, chopped

Combine all ingredients except eggs in 3-cup mixing bowl, blend thoroughly; then gently fold in eggs.
Makes 1½ cups.

Bacon-Wrapped Waterchestnuts or Pineapple Chunks

20 waterchestnuts (5-ounce can) or
      pineapple chunks

10 strips thinly-sliced bacon (about ¼ pound),
      cut in half

Wrap each waterchestnut or pineapple chunk in ½ strip bacon and place in shallow baking pan lined with aluminum foil, making certain that bacon end is placed down.

Bake in oven preheated to 400°F. for about 15 minutes.

Makes 20 appetizers.

ALTERNATE: For Bacon-Wrapped Saltine Crackers: Substitute 20 saltines or salt-free cracker squares for waterchestnuts and increase bacon to 20 strips or ½ pound. These may be baked ahead, being careful not to overbake; then reheated before serving.

Dried Beef Rolls

A well-liked old-timer made from reliables you can have on hand to help out on unexpected occasions. Make Leftover Beef and Noodle Casserole (p. 71) with leftover dried beef.

3 tablespoons whipped cottage cheese,
      low-fat cottage cheese, sour cream,
      sour cream substitute, yogurt,
      or cream cheese

1 small green onion, minced

⅛ teaspoon Worcestershire sauce or diet
      Worcestershire sauce

¼ teaspoon prepared horseradish

6 slices dried beef

Mix together cottage cheese, onion, Worcestershire sauce, and horseradish in small bowl or cup.

Spread about 1½ teaspoonfuls of cheese mixture over each slice of dried beef. Roll-up like jelly roll; then cut in half.

Makes 12 appetizers.

Cheese Spread

Keeps well under refrigeration and makes a nice gift, too. Grated cheese comes in packages if you need it for convenience.

- 3 ounces or ⅓ cup cream cheese or lowered-fat cream cheese
- 3 ounces or ⅓ cup grated cheddar or pimiento cheese, gently packed into cup
- Dash cayenne pepper
- ¼ teaspoon prepared mustard
- ¼ teaspoon garlic salt or ⅛ teaspoon garlic powder
- ¼ teaspoon grated orange rind (optional, but a very distinguishing and worthwhile addition)
- 2 tablespoons dry white wine, vermouth, or beer
- ¼ cup finely chopped green olives stuffed with pimiento (optional)

Cream cheeses together in 2-cup bowl; then add remaining ingredients except olives and mix very well. Add olives.

Makes 1 cup.

Cheese Cocktail Wafers

A very unexpected and delicious treat served as an appetizer or with special luncheon salad.

1½ cups unsifted flour

¼ to ½ teaspoon cayenne pepper

¼ teaspoon salt or salt substitute

½ cup butter or margarine

4 ounces sharp cheddar cheese or low-moisture, part-skim cheese, grated

¼ cup finely chopped nuts or waterchestnuts

Mix together flour, cayenne pepper, and salt in 3-cup bowl. Add butter and blend until smooth; then add cheese and nuts and blend thoroughly. Knead; then form into roll or rolls and wrap in aluminum foil. Refrigerate at least overnight, or freeze until needed.

Slice about ⅜-inch thick and place on cookie sheet.

Bake at 425°F. for 10 minutes and remove from cookie sheet immediately.

Makes about 2 dozen.

Low-Calorie Clam Dip

1 cup sour cream substitute or yogurt

6½-ounce can minced clams

1 to 2 tablespoons liquid from clams

Few drops Tabasco

½ teaspoon Worcestershire sauce or diet Worcestershire sauce

Dash garlic salt or powder

Drain clams, reserving liquid.

Mix together clams and sour cream substitute in 2-cup bowl. Add liquid from clams beginning with 1 tablespoon and adding more liquid until mixture is right consistency for dip.

Serve with cherry tomatoes, cauliflowerettes, celery, cucumber and zucchini sticks, or potato chips. **Makes 1½ cups.**

ALTERNATE: For Low-Calorie Olive Dip: Substitute ⅓ cup chopped green olives stuffed with pimiento for clams and milk for clam liquid.

Eggplant Caviar

1 small eggplant

½ cup onion, chopped fine

⅔ cup green pepper, chopped fine

1 very small clove garlic, minced

1 tablespoon olive or cooking oil

½ teaspoon salt or salt substitute

⅛ teaspoon pepper

½ teaspoon sugar or granulated sugar
  replacement

1 small tomato, finely chopped, or
  1 tablespoon tomato paste

1 tablespoon lemon juice or dry white wine

Place washed, whole eggplant in shallow baking dish;
then bake at 400°F. for 1 hour, or until eggplant is
soft.

Cook onion, green pepper, and garlic in olive oil in
1-quart sauce pan until soft.

Peel and cut up eggplant; then add to onion and
green pepper. Add salt, pepper, sugar, tomato, and
lemon juice and cook over medium-low heat until
mixture is consistency of mashed potatoes. Pour into
bowl and refrigerate until well chilled.

Serve with party rye bread or rye crackers.

Makes about 1½ cups.

Seafood Cocktail Sauce

Serve as a sauce for shrimp and oysters or over sea-food mixed with celery as first course.

½ cup chili sauce or diet chili sauce

2 to 3 tablespoons lemon juice

½ teaspoon Worcestershire sauce or diet Worcestershire sauce

1 teaspoon minced onion or ⅛ teaspoon onion salt

Few drops Tabasco

Combine all ingredients in small bowl or cup and mix well.

Makes 1 cup.

Swedish Meat Balls

Ah, the subtle flavor and the toothsome crunchiness of that silent star performer, the water chestnut, is the secret to this hors d'oeuvre or meat course extraordinaire.

¾ pound lean ground beef

½ cup fresh bread crumbs

⅓ cup finely chopped water chestnuts

1 beaten egg, ¼ cup frozen egg substitute, or 2 tablespoons powdered egg substitute mixed with 2½ tablespoons water

⅞ cup milk or skim, 2% fat or reconstituted instant dry milk

2 teaspoons minced onion

⅛ teaspoon ground mace or nutmeg

⅛ teaspoon ground allspice

½ teaspoon salt or salt substitute

⅛ teaspoon pepper

Continued on following page

SWEDISH MEAT BALLS — *Continued*

1   teaspoon instant beef bouillon, bottled brown bouquet sauce or bouillon cube

1   tablespoon meat drippings

1   tablespoon flour

½   cup sauterne

Crumble beef into 1-quart mixing bowl; then add bread crumbs and water chestnuts.

Mix together beaten egg, ½ cup milk, onion, mace, allspice, salt, and pepper in small bowl or cup. Pour over meat and blend thoroughly.

Line shallow baking pan with aluminum foil.

Form meat into 1-inch balls and place on foil. Broil, turning to brown all sides evenly.

Place beef bouillon and 1 tablespoon of drippings from meat in 1-quart saucepan; then add flour and stir until smooth. Add remaining ⅓ cup milk and sauterne; then cook over medium heat, stirring continually, until thickened. Return meat balls to gravy; then cover and simmer about 20 minutes, or put meat balls and gravy in casserole with cover and bake at 325°F. for 40 minutes.

Makes 20 meat balls for appetizers or 4 servings for meat course.

Beverages

Cafe au Chocolat Mix

This tangy coffee/cocoa mix yields 30 individual servings. Keep a jarful handy.

6 tablespoons instant coffee or
   decaffeinated coffee

4 tablespoons cocoa or carob powder

Boiling water

Sugar, granulated sugar replacement, or
   saccharin

Mix together instant coffee and cocoa in ½-pint jar with lid.

To serve Cafe au Chocolat: Mix 1 teaspoon of coffee and cocoa mix with 5 ounces boiling water for each serving. Sugar, sugar replacement, or saccharin may be added to taste.

Makes 30 cups.

Hot Spiced Cider or Wine

Make this wonderful winter warmer in your electric percolator.

4 cups apple cider, apple or grape juice, or
     red wine

2 cinnamon sticks

1 teaspoon whole cloves

½-inch piece bay leaf (optional)

Pour cider, juice, or wine into electric percolator or 2-quart saucepan. Place cinnamon sticks, cloves, and bay leaf in percolator basket or add to liquid in saucepan.

Plug in coffemaker and let it go through regular cycle or simmer liquid and spices over low heat for 30 minutes. Remove spices and serve. Makes four 8-ounce servings or eight 4-ounce servings depending upon whether mugs, coffee cups, or punch cups are being used.

Irish Coffee

1½ teaspoons sugar or granulated sugar
       replacement

1½ teaspoons instant coffee or
       decaffeinated coffee

1½ ounces Irish whiskey

     Boiling water

1½ tablespoons whipped low-calorie dessert
       topping or whipped cream

Mix sugar and coffee together in bottom of stemmed goblet or Irish coffee glass. Add Irish whiskey and fill glass to within ½-inch of top with boiling water. Top with whipped topping.

   1 serving.

Cranberry Special

⅓ cup cranberry juice

1 cup chilled club soda

⅓ cup lemon ice or sherbet

Combine cranberry juice and club soda in 2-cup pitcher; then divide into two 10-inch glasses. Add half of lemon ice to each, stir and serve at once.

2 servings.

Fruit Punch

It's easy to make more of this for a large group. Canned, frozen, or freshly bottled juices may be used.

   2 teaspoons dried mint flakes

  ½ cup water

  ¼ cup sugar or sugar replacement

     Juice of 1 lemon

1 ¼ cups pineapple juice

1 ¼ cups grapefruit juice

  ¾ cup apricot, passion fruit, or guava nectar

   1 cup club soda (optional)

Boil mint flakes, water, and sugar together for 5 minutes in 1-cup saucepan. Cool.

Combine mint syrup with remaining ingredients in 1 ½ -quart pitcher or container. Refrigerate, if desired, or pour over ice and serve.

Makes about five 8-ounce servings, depending upon whether sparkling water is used.

ALTERNATE: 8 ounces rum, gin, vodka or ⅕-quart white wine may be added, if desired.

Russian Tea Mix

Something special to have on hand. Good hot or cold and an extra nice morning booster if you hate fuss . . . and/or coffee.

1¼ cups orange-flavored instant breakfast
      drink

⅓ cup instant tea

½ cup sugar or granulated sugar replacement

½ teaspoon ground cinnamon

¼ teaspoon ground cloves

⅛ teaspoon salt or salt substitute

Combine all ingredients in 1-pint jar with lid. Screw on top and shake until well blended.
Makes 2 cups.

For hot tea: Mix 2 teaspoons Russian Tea Mix with 6 ounces boiling water. For iced tea: Mix 4 teaspoons Russian Tea Mix with 8 to 10 ounces water; then add ice.

Summer Refresher

2 cups orange juice

1 cup cold tea

Juice of 1 lemon

¼ to ½ cup sugar or granulated sugar
   replacement, depending on desired
   sweetness

12 ounces lemon-lime carbonated beverage
   or low-calorie lemon-lime carbonated
   beverage

Combine all ingredients in 1½-quart pitcher or container and stir until sugar is dissolved. Refrigerate, if desired, or pour over ice and serve.

Makes four 8-ounce servings.

ALTERNATE: 6 to 8 ounces vodka or gin may be added, if desired.

Wine Cooler

A favorite of an 85 years young girl of the golden age.

½ cup claret or port wine

 3 cups lemon-lime carbonated beverage or
      low-calorie lemon-lime carbonated
      beverage

Mix wine and lemon-lime beverage together in 1-quart
pitcher. Pour over ice and serve.

   4 servings.

ALTERNATE: For Fresh Lemon Wine Cooler: Substitute ⅓ cup sugar or granulated sugar replacement
and the juice of 3 lemons mixed with 3 cups club soda
for the lemon-lime carbonated beverage.

SOUPS

Bone-Bag Soup

Here is a nearly no-cost meal. Save any kind of bones (lamb, chicken, beef, pork) in a plastic bag in the freezer. At the same time, keep a container in the refrigerator for leftover meats, vegetables, gravies, and cooking water from vegetables. Put it all together and you have a superlative soup.

1 bag of bones equivalent to 3 beef ribs and 2 chop bones; or 1 lamb-leg bone, a chop bone, and 2 chicken bones

¼ pound stew meat or beef shank if more meat is desired

3 cups leftover cooking liquids, consommé, Bouillon (p. 27), or water (or any combination to make 3 cups)

1 carrot, diced

1 large celery stalk, cut-up

1 small onion, chopped

1 teaspoon salt or salt substitute

⅛ teaspoon pepper or 2 peppercorns

Continued on following page

BONE-BAG SOUP — *Continued*

1 small clove garlic, minced, or
⅛ teaspoon garlic powder

1 whole clove or ⅛ teaspoon ground cloves

½-inch piece bay leaf

1 cup frozen mixed vegetables or 1 cup canned
or fresh vegetables of choice

1 tablespoon rice or barley

1 small potato, diced (optional)

8-ounce can tomato sauce or stewed tomatoes
or 1 cup cut-up fresh tomatoes

Place bones, meat, and liquids in 2-quart heavy sauce-pan with cover; then add carrot, celery, onions, salt, pepper, garlic, cloves, and bay leaf. Simmer over low heat for 2 hours.

Refrigerate; then skim off fat and pick meat from bones. Return meat to soup stock.

Add mixed vegetables, rice or barley, potato, and tomatoes to soup stock and simmer over low heat until vegetables are tender.

Makes 1 to 1½ quarts.

Bouillon (BROWN STOCK)

To be used in any recipe calling for bouillon or consommé and as a rich soup base. Especially good for dieters as it may be made salt-free.

- 1 pound beef shank
- 1½ quarts water
- 1 medium carrot, scraped and quartered
- ¾ cup sliced onion (about 1 medium)
- 1 medium clove garlic, cut in half
- 3 peppercorns or ¼ teaspoon pepper
- ½ bay leaf
- 1 teaspoon dried parsley flakes or
  1 tablespoon fresh chopped parsley
- 1 teaspoon salt or salt substitute
- 2 whole cloves (optional)
- ¼ teaspoon dried thyme (optional)

Combine all ingredients in 2-quart saucepan with cover. Bring to boil and skim off foam. Reduce heat to low and simmer for 3½ hours. Remove from heat; then remove bones, meat, and larger pieces of vegetables with slotted spoon and place in bowl.

Pour broth through sieve into 2-quart bowl; then pour clear broth into 1-quart jar, seal, and refrigerate. When thoroughly chilled remove fat from top of jar. Keeps well in refrigerator or freezer. **Makes 1 quart.**

Make Beef Stew (p 84), Beef Hash (p. 70), Stroganoff from Leftover Beef (p. 85), Leftover Roast Beef in Sauce with Spaghetti (p. 73), or Leftover Beef and Noodle Casserole (p. 71) from meat remaining after bouillon is made.

Corn Chowder

17-ounce can cream-style corn

1 teaspoon instant chicken bouillon or
1 chicken bouillon cube

¾ cup milk or skim, 2% fat or
reconstituted instant dry milk

1 teaspoon Worcestershire sauce or
diet Worcestershire sauce

Few grains pepper

Few drops Tabasco

⅛ teaspoon onion salt or 1 teaspoon minced
onion

1 teaspoon imitation bacon flavored bits
(optional)

Combine all ingredients in 3-cup saucepan and cook over medium-low heat, but do not boil.
  2 servings.

Ham Bone Soup

⅓ cup dried lima or navy beans

¼ cup split green peas

1 tablespoon barley

1 tablespoon rice

3 cups water

1 ham bone or 1-pound cooked ham shank

1 onion, chopped

¼ cup chopped celery

½ cup chopped carrots

1 chopped tomato, peeled

½ teaspoon sugar or sugar replacement

½ teaspoon salt or salt substitute

Few grains pepper

Put beans, peas, barley, and rice in 2-quart saucepan with cover; then add water and cook, covered, for 45 minutes. Add ham, onion, celery, carrots, tomato, sugar, salt, pepper, and more water, if necessary. Cook 1½ hours, or until beans are tender.

4 servings.

ALTERNATE: For Split Pea Soup: Add ¾ cup additional green split peas and omit beans, barley, and rice.

Onion Soup

The marriage of butter and oil for browning was made in heaven.

1 tablespoon butter or margarine

1 tablespoon cooking oil

1 cup sliced onion (1 large)

1 teaspoon sugar or granulated sugar replacement

1 cup Bouillon (Brown Stock, p. 27), canned bouillon, or 1 teaspoon beef-flavored instant bouillon or 1 bouillon cube mixed with 1 cup water

½ teaspoon Worcestershire sauce or diet Worcestershire sauce

¼ teaspoon salt or salt substitute

⅛ teaspoon pepper

3 tablespoons red wine (Burgundy or Port are good)

2 slices crusty French bread, toast, or rolls

Grated Parmesan cheese

ONION SOUP — *Continued*

Blend butter and oil in 3-cup saucepan; then add onion and sugar. Stir continually as onions cook and sugar caramelizes, scraping bottom of pan frequently. When onions are very soft and golden brown, add bouillon, Worcestershire sauce, salt, pepper, and wine. Simmer for 15 minutes, or more, if desired.

Pour soup into two bowls or cups, arrange slice of bread on each; then sprinkle generously with grated Parmesan cheese.

Broil for few minutes, or just until cheese is lightly browned.

2 servings.

Baked Onion Soup au Gratin

This is one of those cooking stories with a surprise ending. It's a sure thing that it will be a repeat at your table, and it can be doubled, tripled, et cetera.

　　1-serving envelope onion soup mix or 1 cup
　　　　Onion Soup (p. 30)

¾　cup boiling water (if using soup mix)

1　Holland rusk or piece of dried French,
　　　　Italian, or sourdough bread

　　Grated Parmesan cheese

Combine onion soup mix with boiling water in small bowl or measuring cup.

　　Place rusk or dried bread in casserole; then pour soup over top.

　　Bake at 350°F. for 40 minutes; remove before last 10 minutes of baking and sprinkle generously with Parmesan cheese, then return to oven to finish cooking time.

　　1 serving.

Potato Soup

1½ cups water
1½ cups diced potatoes (1 medium)
 ½ cup diced celery
 ¼ cup finely chopped onion
 ¼ cup diced bacon, Canadian bacon, or ham
  1 teaspoon salt or salt substitute
     Few grains pepper
 ¾ cup milk or skim, 2% fat or reconstituted
     instant dry milk
 ¼ teaspoon Worcestershire sauce or diet
     Worcestershire sauce
     Few drops Tabasco (optional)
  1 tablespoon butter or margarine

Put water into 1-quart saucepan with cover; then add potatoes, celery, onion, bacon, salt, and pepper. Cover and cook over low heat until vegetables are tender. Pour liquid into small bowl and set aside. Mash vegetables with potato masher or spoon, or blend in electric blender; then return liquid to vegetables.

Add milk, Worcestershire sauce, Tabasco, and butter. Heat over medium-low heat, but do not boil.

2 servings.

ALTERNATE: For Clam Chowder: Add 6½-ounce can of clams and liquid mixed with 2 teaspoons flour.

Cream of Tomato Soup

This is a thrifty, simple soup to make and will carefully accommodate those on low-sodium diets for whom the packaged and canned tomato soups are forbidden. Who cares? This tastes far better . . . and is almost as convenient.

1½ tablespoons butter or margarine

1½ tablespoons flour

 ¼ teaspoon salt or salt substitute

     Few grains pepper

1½ cups milk or skim, 2% fat or reconstituted
     instant dry milk

2½ cups cut-up fresh tomatoes

 1 tablespoon minced onion

     Dash dried basil

     Dash ground cloves

 ⅛ teaspoon baking soda or low-sodium
     substitute

CREAM OF TOMATO SOUP — *Continued*

Melt butter in 1-quart saucepan; then stir in flour, salt, and pepper. Add milk all at once and cook over me-dium-low heat until sauce is thickened. Set aside.

Cook tomatoes with onion, basil, and cloves until done; then add soda.

Place sieve over saucepan with white sauce. Pour tomatoes into sieve and press with spoon until all pulp has been pushed through sieve. Stir tomatoes into white sauce until smooth.

Return to medium-low heat and heat, but do not boil. If soup curdles, beat smooth with spoon or egg beater. Keeps well in refrigerator or freezer.

3 to 4 servings.

Notes:

Instant Tomato-Onion Soup

If you are on a salt- or sugar-restricted diet, packaged soup mix will not be allowed in most cases. Don't despair, you can make your own concoction from low-sodium tomato soup, cooked onions, and bottled brown bouquet sauce.

1-serving envelope cream of tomato soup mix
  or 1 cup Cream of Tomato Soup (p. 34)

1-serving envelope onion soup mix or 1 cup
  Onion Soup (p. 30)

1 cup boiling water (if using soup mix)

Combine tomato and onion soup mixes in 2-cup saucepan; then add boiling water. Simmer a few minutes over low heat.

Makes 1 bowl or 2 cups of soup.

FISH
and
Shellfish

Baked Fillet of Fish

8-ounce fillet of snapper, halibut, kingfish,
and the like

Salt or salt substitute

Pepper

1 to 1½ slices Swiss or low-moisture,
part-skim cheese

¼ cup sour cream, sour cream
substitute, or yogurt

Tomato slice (optional)

Green pepper ring (optional)

Select a baking dish with a cover that will best accommodate fillet (or fillets without overlapping).

Grease dish and arrange fish in bottom. Sprinkle with salt and pepper; then place piece of cheese over each fillet and sprinkle again with pepper. Gently cover surface with sour cream; top with tomato slice and pepper ring. Cover.

Bake at 300°F. for about 35 minutes, or until fish flakes with a fork (larger or thicker fillets require 5 to 10 minutes longer).

1 serving.

Favorite Broiled Fish

Although it originated with cooking mahi mahi, this traditional Hawaiian method plays no favorites among kinds of fish. Recipe is easily adjusted for more or fewer than two.

1 pound frozen or fresh fillet of sole, perch, flounder, snapper, mahi mahi and the like

1 tablespoon mayonnaise or diet mayonnaise

Lemon pepper or pepper

Seasoned salt or seasoned salt substitute

Paprika (optional)

Grated Parmesan cheese (optional)

Line flat baking dish or pan with 24-inch piece of aluminum foil. Arrange fillets on foil.

Thinly coat fillets with mayonnaise; then sprinkle alternately with pepper, salt, paprika, and cheese.

Fold ends of foil to middle and seal; then fold and seal remaining sides.

Broil about 15 minutes or until fillets are puffy and flake with fork. Turn back foil and broil few minutes until lightly browned.

2 servings.

Florida-Style Fish Fillet

Of all the ways to fix fish this has to be one of the most delicious. Don't let the unusual inclusion of brown gravy deter you.

2 finely chopped green onions and tops

1 pound fillet of red snapper, halibut, grouper, haddock, and the like

1 tablespoon olive oil

½ teaspoon salt or salt substitute

Few grains pepper

½ cup leftover, or canned brown gravy, or Brown Gravy (p. 65)

¼ cup dry white wine

2 teaspoons dried sweet pepper or 2 tablespoons chopped green pepper

Select a baking dish that will best accommodate fillet (or fillets without overlapping).

Line dish with aluminum foil; then sprinkle onions evenly over bottom. Arrange fillets over onions.

Mix together olive oil, salt, pepper, gravy, and wine in small bowl or cup. Spoon mixture over fish and sprinkle green pepper on top.

Bake at 350°F. for about 30 minutes or until fish flakes with fork.

2 servings.

Poached Fish Fillets or Steaks with Mustard Sauce

½ cup water

 1 tablespoon lemon juice

¼ cup chopped onion or 1 green onion, chopped

½-inch piece bay leaf

½ teaspoon salt or salt substitute

⅛ teaspoon pepper

 8-ounce fish fillet or steak

 2 teaspoons cooking oil

 2 teaspoons flour

 2 teaspoons prepared mustard

½ cup strained liquid from fish

Select a saucepan with cover that will best accommodate fish fillets or steaks.

Place water, lemon juice, onion, bay leaf, salt, and pepper in saucepan; bring to boil over low heat and simmer for 5 minutes. Add fish, cover and simmer 10 to 15 minutes or until fish flakes with a fork. Remove fish, cover with foil, and keep warm while making mustard sauce.

Mix together cooking oil, flour, and mustard in small saucepan. Add stock, using, if necessary, some milk to make ½ cup. Cook, stirring constantly, until thickened. Pour sauce over fish.

2 servings.

Oysters in Casserole

⅔ cup saltine cracker crumbs or salt-free cracker crumbs or herb-seasoned packaged stuffing

½ cup milk or skim, 2% fat or reconstituted instant dry milk

1 beaten egg, ¼ cup frozen egg substitute, or 2 tablespoons powdered egg substitute mixed with 2½ tablespoons water

½ pint oysters

½ cup corn niblets

1 tablespoon butter or margarine

1 tablespoon minced onion

¼ teaspoon salt

Dash of Tabasco

¼ cup shredded American, cheddar, or 99% fat-free cheese (optional)

Mix together crackers, milk, and eggs in 2-cup bowl; set aside for 20 minutes. Add remaining ingredients except cheese and pour into greased 3-cup casserole. Sprinkle with cheese.

Bake in oven preheated to 350°F. for 35 to 40 minutes. **2 servings.**

ALTERNATE: For clams in Casserole: Substitute 6½-ounce can clams, drained, for oysters.

Oyster Stew

A ten minute wonder!

- 1　green onion and top, finely chopped
- 1　tablespoon butter or margarine
- 10　ounces fresh or fresh frozen oysters and liquid
- 1½　cups milk or skim, 2% fat or reconstituted instant dry milk
- ¼　teaspoon salt or salt substitute
- Few grains pepper
- Dash cayenne pepper or paprika

Cook onions in butter in 1-quart saucepan. Add oysters and liquid; bring just to boiling point. Add milk, salt, pepper, and cayenne pepper. Heat, but do not boil. Ready to serve when oysters rise to surface or when edges of oysters begin to curl.

2 servings.

Scallacado (Baked Scallops and Avocado)

Credit the French with a practical innovation called "beurre manié." It is equal amounts of flour and butter kneaded together and formed into balls, so when a gravy, sauce, stew, or soup needs thickening, there is an immediate answer by quickly dropping a "beurre manié" into the liquid.

2 teaspoons butter or margarine

2 teaspoons flour

⅓ cup milk or skim, 2% fat or
    reconstituted instant dry milk

⅛ teaspoon salt

   Few grains pepper

1 teaspoon finely minced onion

1 tablespoon white wine or 1 teaspoon
    lemon juice

1½ tablespoons grated Parmesan cheese

1 large avocado

8 to 10 frozen fried sea scallops

Continued on following page

SCALLACADO (BAKED SCALLOPS AND AVOCADO) — *Continued*

Mix together butter and flour (beurre manié) in 1-cup saucepan until smooth. Add milk, salt, pepper, and onion; then cook over medium-low heat until thickened. Stir in wine and cheese; cook until well-blended. Set aside.

Cut avocado in half and remove seed. Set each avocado half on an 8-inch square piece aluminum foil. Fold foil around avocado to act as stabilizer underneath narrow end.

Place one scallop in avocado center; spoon sauce on top. Arrange remaining 3 or 4 scallops on top and around center scallop. Spoon sauce over each scallop, being careful that it does not run off sides.

Bake at 350°F. for about 30 minutes.

2 servings.

ALTERNATE I: For Shrimp-filled Avocado: Substitute fried shrimp for scallops.

ALTERNATE II: For Clam-filled Avocado: Substitute fried clams for scallops.

Shrimp Casserole

Plastic bags of the smallest frozen cooked shrimp are a convenient and economical investment as a few may be used at a time and the remainder returned to the freezer for another day.

¾ cup uncooked spaghetti or thin noodles broken into small pieces

⅔ cup cream of mushroom soup or 1-serving envelope instant cream of mushroom soup mix and ⅓ cup water

1 tablespoon minced onion

Few grains pepper

½ teaspoon dried sweet pepper or 1 tablespoon minced green pepper

6 ounces or ¾ cup cooked shrimp, drained and dried with paper towelling

⅓ cup finely diced cheddar or 99% fat-free cheese

⅓ cup green peas (optional)

Continued on following page

SHRIMP CASSEROLE — *Continued*

Cook spaghetti or noodles in 3-cup saucepan according to package directions just until tender. Drain.

Mix soup with spaghetti; then add onion, pepper, sweet pepper, shrimp, cheese, and peas. Pour into greased 2-cup casserole.

Bake at 350°F. for 30 minutes.

2 servings.

ALTERNATE I: For Crabmeat Casserole: Substitute a 7½-ounce can crabmeat for shrimp and add 1 hard-boiled egg, diced, and 1 tablespoon chopped pimiento.

ALTERNATE II: For Chicken Casserole: Substitute cooked, diced chicken for shrimp and cream of chicken soup for mushroom soup.

ALTERNATE III: For Clam Casserole: Substitute a 6½-ounce can minced clams, drained, for shrimp.

Shrimp Creole

1 tablespoon minced onion or 1 teaspoon instant chopped onion

1 teaspoon butter, margarine, cooking or olive oil

1 tablespoon minced green pepper or 1 teaspoon dried sweet pepper

¼ cup diced celery

½ cup tomato sauce

⅛ teaspoon garlic powder

½ teaspoon sugar or granulated sugar replacement

¼ teaspoon salt or salt substitute

⅛ teaspoon dried thyme

½-inch piece bay leaf (optional)

2 to 4 ounces cooked shrimp (very small are especially suitable)

1 to 1½ cups cooked rice

Continued on following page

SHRIMP CREOLE — *Continued*

Cook onions in butter in 2-cup saucepan until soft. Add green pepper, celery, tomato sauce, garlic powder, sugar, salt, thyme, and bay leaf. Simmer over very low heat until celery is tender; then add shrimp and cook 5 to 10 minutes more, depending on size of shrimp.

Remove bay leaf and spoon shrimp mixture over rice.

2 servings.

ALTERNATE: For Leftover Lamb Creole : Substitute ½ cup cooked, diced lamb for shrimp.

Notes:

Sweet and Sour Shrimp

To meet low-sodium diet requirements, diet Worcestershire sauce is a good substitute for soy sauce.

½ cup boiling water

2 to 3 tablespoons uncooked rice

¼ teaspoon salt or salt substitute

½ cup pineapple juice

½ teaspoon soy sauce or diet
   Worcestershire sauce

1 teaspoon cornstarch

Dash garlic salt or powder

Dash ground ginger

1 small green onion and top, sliced diagonally

1 small celery stalk, sliced diagonally

2 teaspoons cooking oil

¼ cup pineapple chunks

½ cup cooked shrimp, drained and dried with
   paper towelling

Continued on following page

SWEET AND SOUR SHRIMP—*Continued*

Bring water to boil in 2-cup saucepan with cover; add rice and salt. Cook until rice is tender.

Meanwhile, in small bowl or cup mix together pineapple juice, soy sauce, cornstarch, garlic salt, and ginger; set aside.

Cook onion and celery in cooking oil in 2-cup saucepan until soft. Add cornstarch mixture; stir well and add pineapple chunks and shrimp. Cook until sauce is thickened and clear, but do not overcook. Serve over rice.

1 serving.

ALTERNATE I: For Sweet and Sour Pork: Substitute ½ to ¾ cup sliced and quickly browned pork tenderloin or steak for shrimp.

ALTERNATE II: For Sweet and Sour Beef: Substitute ½ to ¾ cup sliced and quickly browned beef steak or tenderloin for shrimp.

Individual Tuna Casserole

3¼-ounce can oil- or water-packed tuna

½ cup fresh bread crumbs

1 tablespoon minced onion or ¼ teaspoon instant chopped onion

¼ cup minced celery

1 tablespoon mayonnaise, cottage cheese, yogurt, or sour cream or diet mayonnaise, low-fat cottage cheese, or sour cream substitute

⅛ teaspoon salt or salt substitute

Few grains pepper

Slice of American, cheddar, or 99% fat-free cheese

Rinse tuna in cold water and drain; then flake into 3-cup bowl. Blend in bread, celery, onion, mayonnaise, salt, and pepper.

Pour tuna mixture into lightly greased 1½-cup baking dish and top with cheese.

Bake in oven preheated to 325°F. for 20 minutes.

1 serving.

ALTERNATE I: Substitute salmon for tuna.

ALTERNATE II: Substitute leftover cooked fish for tuna.

Tuna or Salmon Casserole

3¼-ounce can oil- or water-packed tuna or
    salmon

¾ cup cooked elbow macaroni

  2-ounce can mushroom stems and pieces,
    drained

¼ cup sliced green olives stuffed with
    pimiento

¼ cup chopped green pepper

½ cup sour cream, sour cream
    substitute, or yogurt

½ cup grated American, cheddar, or 99%
    fat-free cheese

Drain and flake tuna or salmon into 3-cup mixing bowl.
Add remaining ingredients except cheese. Spread in
buttered 2-cup casserole and sprinkle with cheese.

   Bake in oven preheated to 350°F. for 25 to 30
minutes.

   1 serving.

Party Tuna or Salmon

Here is lots of impact for very little work. Recipe multiplies easily to serve from one to ten or twenty.

3¼-ounce can oil- or water-packed tuna or
   salmon

3 to 4 cooked frozen or canned artichoke
   hearts

¼ cup sour cream, sour cream
   substitute, or yogurt

1 teaspoon minced onion or chives or
   freeze dried chives

⅛ teaspoon salt or salt substitute

Few grains pepper

1 tablespoon finely chopped dill pickle or
   green olives (optional)

Paprika

Continued on following page.

PARTY TUNA OR SALMON — *Continued*

Drain and flake tuna. (Rinse first in cold water, if desired.)

Grease individual baking shell or dish; then arrange artichoke hearts in bottom. Heap flaked fish over artichoke hearts.

Mix together sour cream, onion or chives, salt, pepper, and dill pickle or green olives in small bowl or cup. Spoon mixture over tuna and sprinkle with paprika.

Bake at 350°F. for about 30 minutes or until bubbling hot.

1 serving.

ALTERNATE: Substitute ½ cup cooked green peas or mixed vegetables for artichoke hearts.

BEEF

Beef Pinwheel

Looking for a helpmate? Keep the 1-cup size envelope of various gravy mixes on your cupboard shelf for this and many other dishes.

4-ounce package refrigerated biscuits or
    1 recipe Biscuits (p. 271)
1 tablespoon mayonnaise, diet mayonnaise,
    butter, or margarine
1 tablespoon catsup or diet catsup
½ teaspoon prepared mustard
2 tablespoons chopped onion
½ teaspoon salt or salt substitute
1 teaspoon dried parsley
1 tablespoon grated Parmesan cheese
    (optional)
1 cup Beef Gravy (p. 65), mushroom soup,
    1 envelope (1-cup size) brown gravy
    mix made according to package directions
½ pound very lean ground beef or
    finely diced cubed steak
¼ cup very finely diced Swiss cheese or
    low-moisture, part-skim cheese

Roll out biscuit dough on floured board into ⅛-inch thick, 8½ x 6½-inch rectangle.

Mix together mayonnaise, catsup, mustard, onion, salt, parsley, Parmesan cheese, and gravy; then add meat and Swiss cheese and mix very well.

Spread meat mixture over rolled-out dough and roll-up like jelly roll.

Bake in oven preheated to 400°F. for 25 minutes. **2 servings.**

Oven Baked Corned Beef Brisket or Round

You will have corned beef left over to make Corned Beef Casserole (p. 62) and extra-good sandwiches.

2- to 3-pound piece corned beef brisket or
    round

2 peppercorns

1 small apple or orange or 2 tablespoons
    concentrated orange juice

½-inch piece bay leaf

1 small clove garlic, cut in half

2 whole cloves

1 cup water

1 carrot

1 onion

1 small potato

1 turnip

1 cabbage wedge

OVEN BAKED CORNED BEEF
BRISKET OR ROUND — *Continued*

Trim most of fat from corned beef; rinse in cold water and place in 2-quart baking dish with cover. Add peppercorns, apple, bay leaf, garlic, cloves, and water. Cover and bake at 325°F. for 1½ hours.

Add vegetables; cover and cook for 1½ to 2 hours, or until fork tender.

2 servings, plus corned beef left over for sandwiches, etc.

ALTERNATE: For Oven Baked Corned Beef Tongue: Substitute corned beef tongue for corned beef.

Notes:

Corned Beef Casserole

There is a long and a short version of this tried and true friend.

½ cup uncooked noodles

Boiling water

¼ teaspoon salt or salt substitute

¼ cup finely chopped onion

1 very small clove garlic, minced (optional)

¼ cup finely chopped celery

¼ cup finely chopped green pepper

2 teaspoons cooking oil

½ to ¾ cup cubed canned or leftover corned beef

½ cup cream of chicken soup, sour cream, or sour cream substitute

⅛ teaspoon dry mustard (optional)

Few grains pepper

⅓ cup American, cheddar, or 99% fat-free cheese

Bread crumbs (optional)

CORNED BEEF CASSEROLE — *Continued*

Cook noodles in boiling water with salt in 2-cup sauce-pan just until tender. Drain and set aside.

Cook onion, garlic, celery, and green pepper in cooking oil in 1-quart saucepan or skillet. When vegetables are tender, but not brown, add corned beef.

Mix together soup, mustard, pepper, and cheese; then add to corned beef and blend well. Gently fold in noodles and pour into greased 3-cup casserole. Sprinkle with bread crumbs.

Bake at 350°F. for 30 to 40 minutes or until bubbling hot.

2 servings.

ALTERNATE I: For Quick and Easy Corned Beef Casserole: Substitute 1 teaspoon dried chopped onion for onion; ⅛ teaspoon garlic powder for garlic; 1 teaspoon dried sweet pepper for green pepper, and cream of celery soup for chicken soup or sour cream, and omit celery.

ALTERNATE II: For Cooked Ham or Bologna Casserole: Substitute cubed ham or bologna for corned beef.

Fat-Free Drippings for Beef Gravy and Sauces

Benefits abound from this easy, but often overlooked procedure. All dieters will welcome a most flavorful solution to making low-fat, low-sodium gravy. All purists will recognize the superior flavor. Those who like lots of results with minimum effort will have their way, too.

2½- to 4-pound beef roast of choice

¼ cup water

Place beef roast in small, shallow baking pan; teflon is superior for this purpose.

Roast meat at 300°F. to 325°F. until desired doneness. Remove meat, scraping juices and browned bits from bottom of roast. Place on aluminum foil or plate to cool before refrigerating.

Add water to pan drippings and refrigerate. When thoroughly chilled, remove all fat particles and pour remaining drippings into small jar to be used as needed for beef gravy or for additional flavoring in stews and the like.

Makes about ⅓ cup, or enough for 5 cups gravy.

Beef Gravy from Fat-Free Drippings

1 tablespoon fat-free beef drippings

1 tablespoon flour

½ cup water, milk or skim, 2% fat or
      reconstituted instant dry milk

¼ teaspoon salt or salt substitute

   Few grains pepper

Combine all ingredients in 1-cup saucepan. Cook over
medium-low heat until thickened.
   Makes ¾ cup gravy.

Creamed Dried Beef

Good for breakfast, lunch, or dinner. Adaptable to ingredients necessary for diets. Even tastes fine without the cheese and wine.

  2 tablespoons margarine or butter

2½ ounces sliced dried beef

  1 tablespoon minced onion or one green onion, chopped

1½ tablespoons flour

  1 cup milk or skim, 2% fat or reconstituted instant dry milk

  2-ounce can mushroom stems and pieces with liquid

  ½ teaspoon dried parsley

  ½ cup grated American, cheddar, or 99% fat-free cheese

  2 tablespoons dry white wine (optional)

CREAMED DRIED BEEF — *Continued*

Melt margarine in 3-cup saucepan. Cut or tear dried beef into small pieces and add to margarine with onion. Cook 3 or 4 minutes. Blend in flour; then gradually add milk, stirring continually. Add mushrooms with liquid and parsley; cook a few minutes longer. Add cheese and stir until melted. Serve over English muffins, toast, rice, or mashed potatoes.

2 servings.

ALTERNATE I: For Creamed Bologna: Substitute ½ cup cut-up bologna for dried beef.

ALTERNATE II: For Creamed Ham: Substitute ½ cup diced, cooked ham for dried beef.

ALTERNATE III: Add 1 hard-cooked egg, diced; ¼ cup sliced ripe olives or pimiento to any of the above.

Ground Beef Casserole

½ pound ground beef chuck

¼ cup chopped onion

¼ cup chopped green pepper

¼ cup chopped celery

1 small clove garlic, minced

1 cup tomato sauce

¼ teaspoon fines herbes or mixed herbs

¾ teaspoon salt or salt substitute

⅛ teaspoon pepper

¼ cup water

¼ cup uncooked elbow macaroni

⅓ cup grated American, cheddar, or 99%
     fat-free cheese

½ cup frozen corn, mixed vegetables, or
     succotash

Brown meat in skillet; then add onion, green pepper, celery, and garlic. Cook, stirring frequently, until vegetables are soft; then add remaining ingredients. Pour into greased 3-cup casserole.

Bake at 350°F. for 45 minutes to 1 hour.

2 to 3 servings.

Unusual Ground Beef Casserole

½ to ¾ pound lean ground beef

 2 tablespoons uncooked rice

½ teaspoon salt or salt substitute

¼ teaspoon pepper

¼ teaspoon dried basil or cumin

⅛ teaspoon garlic powder

½ to ¾ pound lean ground beef

 1-serving envelope cream of tomato soup
 mixed with ⅔ cup boiling water or 1 cup
 tomato sauce or cut-up fresh tomatoes,
 or 1 cup Cream of Tomato Soup (p. 34)

¼ cup chopped onion

½ cup chopped celery

½ cup chopped carrot

¼ cup dry red wine (optional)

Thoroughly mix beef, rice, salt, pepper, basil, and garlic powder in small bowl. Form mixture into two patties.

Brown patties in 7-inch skillet or stove-to-oven casserole with cover; then drain off fat.

In same small bowl, mix together soup and water or tomato sauce, onion, celery, and carrots. Pour over beef patties. Cover.

Bake at 325°F. for 1¼ to 1½ hours.

2 servings.

Beef Hash

If you have been avoiding instant mashed potatoes because of an experience with the earliest product, give them another try; the new, name-brand versions are excellent.

½ cup leftover diced beef roast

½ cup packaged, canned, leftover beef gravy or Beef Gravy (p. 65)

1½ tablespoons instant mashed potatoes mixed with ¼ cup hot water

2 tablespoons milk or skim, 2% fat or reconstituted instant dry milk

1 teaspoon butter or margarine

¼ teaspoon salt or salt substitute

1 teaspoon Worcestershire sauce or diet Worcestershire sauce

½ cup leftover vegetables (optional)

Mix beef with gravy in 2-cup bowl.

Blend instant mashed potatoes with hot water, milk, and butter in small bowl or cup. Add salt, Worcestershire sauce, and vegetables; mix with beef. Pour into 1½-cup casserole.

Bake at 350°F. until warmed through.

1 serving.

Leftover Beef and Noodle Casserole

Two easy procedures will give you full-flavor for gravies: Brown the flour in the oven and use low-calorie, fat-free drippings attained by refrigerating pan juices from roasts, removing the layer of fat that rises to the top and using the resulting liquid as a gravy base. Mix the flour and the rich meat juices together and you really have something special.

¾ cup uncooked noodles
 1 tablespoon margarine or butter
½ cup chopped onion
 2-ounce can mushroom stems and pieces
       with liquid
 1 cup beef gravy or 1 tablespoon flour mixed
       with 1 cup milk or skim, 2% fat or
       reconstituted instant dry milk
½ teaspoon salt or salt substitute
    Few grains pepper
 2 teaspoons Worcestershire sauce or diet
       Worcestershire sauce
    Dash cayenne pepper (optional)
¾ cup diced leftover beef roast

Continued on following page

LEFTOVER BEEF AND NOODLE CASSEROLE — *Continued*

Cook noodles in salted water according to package directions.

Melt margarine in 3-cup stove-to-oven casserole; then add onion and cook until soft. Add mushrooms, gravy or flour mixed with milk, salt, pepper, Worcestershire sauce, cayenne pepper, and beef. Cook until mixture is thickened if using milk and flour, or until hot and bubbling.

Gently fold in cooked noodles; then bake at 325°F. for 30 minutes.

2 servings.

Notes:

Leftover Roast Beef in Sauce with Spaghetti

2 to 3 tablespoons finely chopped onion

2 teaspoons olive or cooking oil

⅛ teaspoon dried oregano

⅛ teaspoon dried basil

8-ounce can stewed tomatoes with onions and green pepper or 7¼-ounce can low-sodium tomato soup or 1-serving envelope cream of tomato soup mix and ⅔ cup of water, or Cream of Tomato Soup (p. 34)

¼ cup chopped ripe olives (optional)

¼ teaspoon garlic salt or dash garlic powder

¼ teaspoon salt or salt substitute

Few grains pepper

1 cup cut-up, leftover roast beef

1 cup uncooked spaghetti

Grated Parmesan cheese

Continued on following page

LEFTOVER ROAST BEEF IN SAUCE WITH SPAGHETTI — *Continued*

Cook onions until soft in olive oil in a 3-cup saucepan with cover; then add oregano and basil. Let herbs cook 2 or 3 minutes and add tomatoes, olives, garlic salt, salt, pepper, and meat. Cover and simmer over low heat until flavors are well blended, adding a little water if sauce seems too thick.

Cook spaghetti according to package directions and drain.

Pour sauce over spaghetti and sprinkle liberally with grated Parmesan cheese.

2 servings.

Notes:

Spiced Meat Loaf

There really isn't much wizardy in those packages of meat loaf mix you see on the supermarket shelf. They are just a few herbs and thickeners. This recipe has all that and more, too.

1 egg, 2 egg whites, or ¼ cup frozen egg substitute

½ cup tomato sauce or ¼ cup milk and ¼ cup catsup or diet catsup

½ teaspoon salt or salt substitute

¼ teaspoon pepper

¼ teaspoon garlic salt with parsley or ⅛ teaspoon garlic powder

½ teaspoon fines herbes

¼ teaspoon dry mustard

1 tablespoon Worcestershire sauce or diet Worcestershire sauce

⅓ cup saltine cracker crumbs or salt-free cracker crumbs

¾ to 1 pound lean ground beef

Continued on following page

SPICED MEAT LOAF — *Continued*

Combine egg, tomato sauce, salt, pepper, garlic salt, fines herbes, mustard, Worcestershire sauce, and cracker crumbs in 3-cup mixing bowl. Add meat and mix very well.

Shape into loaf and place in 7½ x 3½ x 2-inch loaf pan or make two loaves and place in two 6⅛ x 3¾ x 2-inch foil loaf pans (one to be baked, one to be frozen).

Bake at 350°F. for about 40 minutes.

3 servings.

ALTERNATE: For Fast Spiced Meat Loaf: Substitute for the above ingredients: 1 pound meat, ½ cup packaged herb-seasoned dressing, ½ cup tomato sauce, and ¼ cup finely chopped onion.

Notes:

Pasties for Two

A savory meat pie from Great Britain, originally made with venison and game. Great cold for lunch or picnic.

 1 stick pie crust (one-half 11-ounce package) and 2 tablespoons water or 1 recipe for Pie Crust (p. 357)
½ cup or ¼-pound finely diced lean top beef round steak, cubed steak, or lean ground round steak
½ cup finely diced potato
¼ cup finely diced onion
¼ cup finely diced turnip or rutabaga (optional)
¼ teaspoon salt or salt substitute
⅛ teaspoon pepper

Divide pie dough in half and roll out into two 6-inch circles.

Mix remaining ingredients in 3-cup bowl; then spoon half of meat mixture on one half of each pastry circle. Fold remaining half of pastry over first; then seal using a little water around edge. Place on aluminum foil-lined baking dish.

Bake in oven preheated to 425°F. for 15 minutes; reduce heat to 350°F. and bake for 35 to 45 minutes longer.

2 servings.

Peppy Beef Patties

¾ pound lean ground beef

2 tablespoons chili sauce, catsup, or diet catsup

½ teaspoon prepared mustard

⅛ teaspoon onion salt

½ teaspoon Worcestershire sauce or diet Worcestershire sauce

¼ teaspoon salt or salt substitute

Few grains pepper

Dash smoke-flavored salt (optional)

Combine all ingredients in 3-cup mixing bowl and blend thoroughly.

Shape meat into two oval, ½-inch thick patties.

Broil for 5 to 8 minutes on each side. Length of time will depend on type of broiler or outdoor charcoal cooker and desired doneness.

2 servings.

ALTERNATE: For Super Peppy Beef Patties: Make four thin patties from beef mixture. Shape two ¼-inch thick patties of Roquefort, blue, cheddar, or 99% fat-free cheese. Place cheese between two meat patties; seal edges; broil as directed for Peppy Beef Patties.

Individual Pot Roast

The accompanying vegetables should be the kind you like and in a quantity tailored to your appetite.

6-ounce piece boneless beef chuck, English-cut, or round-bone roast

½ lemon

Prepared mustard

Salt or salt substitute

Pepper

Worcestershire sauce or diet Worcestershire sauce

Sugar or granulated sugar replacement

2 tablespoons dry red or white wine (optional)

1 small onion, sliced

1 small carrot, quartered (optional)

1 small potato, halved (optional)

1 turnip (optional)

1 zucchini squash (optional)

Continued on following page

INDIVIDUAL POT ROAST — *Continued*

Trim all fat from meat; then place in center of 12-inch piece aluminum foil in bottom of shallow baking pan.

Rub meat with cut surface of lemon; then spread both sides with mustard.

Preheat broiler; then brown meat on both sides. Remove from oven, squeeze remaining juice from lemon over meat and sprinkle alternately with salt, pepper, Worcestershire sauce, sugar, and wine. Add onion and vegetables of choice. Bring foil over meat and vegetables; seal all edges to make airtight.

Bake at 325°F. for 2½ hours, or until meat is tender.

Notes:

Pot Roast Plus

What does the plus mean? It means you may enjoy the pleasure of having one or two more meals from this succulent meat. Try Stroganoff From Leftover Beef (p. 85), Leftover Beef and Noodle Casserole (p. 71), Leftover Roast Beef in Sauce with Spaghetti (p. 73), and Florida-Style Fish Fillet (p. 41).

2- to 2½-pound boneless chuck roast

1 medium onion, sliced

2 teaspoons beef-flavored instant bouillon or 2 bouillon cubes mixed with ½ cup water or ½ cup bouillon, consommé or Bouillon (p. 27)

¼ teaspoon fines herbes or mixed herbs

1 teaspoon salt or salt substitute

¼ teaspoon pepper

½ cup dry white or red wine or vermouth

2 tablespoons flour

Mashed potatoes, cooked noodles, or rice (½ cup for each serving)

Continued on following page

POT ROAST PLUS — *Continued*

Trim off fat from meat; then place in casserole with cover. Arrange onion slices over top of meat.

Mix bouillon, herbs, salt, pepper, and wine in small bowl or cup. Pour over meat. Cover.

Bake at 350°F. for about 2 hours or until meat is tender, turning meat half way through cooking.

Remove meat and keep warm. Skim off fat from meat juices and measure remaining liquid. Add water to make 2 cups.

Mix flour with a little cold water and stir into liquid. Cook over medium heat, stirring frequently, until thickened. Add more salt and pepper if needed. Serve meat and gravy with cooked noodles, potatoes, or rice.

Notes:

Superb Pot Roast

Do invest in a jar of fines herbes or one of the many good jars of mixed herbs that most reputable spice houses have made available.

2- to 4-pound beef chuck roast
1 tablespoon cooking oil or margarine
Salt or salt substitute
Pepper
Fines herbes or mixed herbs (optional)
½ cup chopped onion
10½-ounce can cream of celery soup or
     10½-ounce can cream of mushroom
     soup and 1 celery stalk, diced
1 teaspoon prepared horseradish
½ cup sour cream, sour cream substitute,
     or yogurt

Trim all fat from meat.

Heat cooking oil in 2-quart stove-to-oven casserole with cover; then brown meat slowly in oil. Sprinkle with salt, pepper, and herbs. Arrange onions on top of meat and pour soup over all. Cover.

Bake at 325°F. for about 3 hours, or until meat is very tender.

Mix horseradish with sour cream in small bowl or cup. Spread over roast; then return to oven, uncovered, for about 5 minutes. Serve with pan gravy.

4 to 8 servings, depending on roast size.

Accommodating Beef Stew

No meat to brown and lots of flexibility in choice of ingredients.

1 pound cubed beef stew meat or round steak

8-ounce can tomato sauce, 7¼-ounce can low-sodium tomato soup, 1-serving envelope cream of tomato soup mix and ⅔ cup water, or 1 cup Cream of Tomato Soup (p. 34)

1 tablespoon instant chopped onion or ¼ cup chopped onion

¾ teaspoon salt or salt substitute

⅛ teaspoon pepper

⅓ cup chopped celery

2 medium carrots cut in ½-inch pieces

1 potato, cut in one-eighths

¼ teaspoon fines herbes, mixed herbs, or thyme

½ cup dry white or red wine, bouillon, consommé, or Bouillon (p. 27), or water

½ slice bread and crust, cubed (1 whole slice French, sourdough, or Italian bread)

Combine all ingredients in 1½-quart baking dish with cover; mixing very well.

Bake at 250°F. for 5 to 6 hours, stirring occasionally. **2 servings.**

Stroganoff from Leftover Beef

Lifesavers for leftovers are bouillon in cans, cubes, and jars; gravies in cans or packets, and bottled brown bouquet sauce with water.

- 2 tablespoons chopped onion
- 1 tablespoon margarine or cooking oil
- ½ cup leftover beef gravy or Beef Gravy (p. 65) or ½ cup bouillon mixed with ½ tablespoon flour
- 1 cup cut-up, leftover roast beef
- 2-ounce can mushroom stems and pieces with liquid
- ⅛ teaspoon dried dill weed
- ¼ teaspoon salt or salt substitute
- Few grains pepper
- ⅓ cup sour cream or sour cream substitute
- 1½ cups cooked rice, mashed potatoes, or noodles

Cook onion in margarine in 6-inch skillet or 2-cup saucepan. Add beef gravy, beef, mushrooms, dill weed, salt, pepper; stir well. Fold in sour cream and heat, but do not boil. Serve immediately over rice, mashed potatoes, or noodles. If to be used later, reheat very carefully over low heat; do not boil.

2 servings.

Boiled Beef Tongue

A good buy because it is all lean meat and is so good cold for luncheon sandwiches.

2½ pounds fresh beef tongue

  1 medium onion, sliced

  4 whole cloves

 ½ teaspoon dried basil

  1 clove garlic, cut in half

  2 teaspoons salt or salt substitute

 ½ teaspoon pepper

Wash tongue; pat dry with paper towelling.

Combine tongue and remaining ingredients with water to cover in 3-quart saucepan with cover.

Cook over low heat for about 3 hours or until tongue is tender. Peel off skin and remove small bones and gristle at end; then serve sliced very thin.

4 to 6 servings.

Liver with Bacon and Onions

¾ pound sliced beef, calves', or pork liver

Juice of ½ lemon

¾ cup chopped onions

2 teaspoons butter, margarine, or cooking oil

4 to 5 strips thin-sliced bacon

Arrange liver in shallow baking pan lined with aluminum foil. Sprinkle with lemon juice. Let stand about 30 minutes.

Meanwhile, cook onions in butter in 6-inch skillet until soft, and set aside.

Arrange bacon over liver; then broil 8 to 10 inches away from element or flame for 10 to 15 minutes without turning.

Spoon onions over meat, or mix 2 to 3 tablespoons drippings from meat with the onions for additional flavor; then spoon over meat and serve.

2 servings.

Liver in Sour Cream

¾ pound sliced beef, calves', or pork liver

1 teaspoon softened butter or margarine

Juice of ½ lemon

Salt or salt substitute

Pepper

¼ cup sour cream or sour cream substitute

1 teaspoon prepared mustard

Arrange liver in shallow baking pan lined with aluminum foil. Spread butter evenly over surface of liver; then sprinkle with lemon juice. Let stand for 30 min.

Broil liver just until lightly browned, on one side only. Remove from heat and sprinkle with salt and pepper. Reduce oven temperature to 350°F.

Mix together sour cream and mustard in small bowl or cup. Spread evenly over liver.

Bake at 350°F. for 10 to 15 minutes, depending on thickness of liver.

2 servings.

LAMB

Broiled Marinated Lamb

One of the tastiest marinades there is. Use it with superb results on chicken, pork, and beef too.

¾ to 1 pound lamb chops or steak, trimmed
       of fat
 1 tablespoon lemon or lime juice
 2 tablespoons soy sauce
       Few grains pepper
⅛ teaspoon garlic powder or ½ clove garlic,
       mashed
 1 tablespoon brown sugar, honey, or
       apple-mint jelly
⅛ teaspoon dry mustard
⅛ teaspoon ground ginger or coriander

Arrange meat in shallow baking dish lined with aluminum foil.

Mix together remaining ingredients in small bowl or cup. Pour over meat. Refrigerate one-half day or overnight.

Broil meat to desired doneness, basting with marinade. **2 servings.**

ALTERNATE I: For Broiled Marinated Chicken: Substitute 2 to 4 chicken breasts, up to 6 thighs, or ½ broiler-fryer for lamb and omit sugar, honey, or jelly.

ALTERNATE II: For Broiled Marinated Pork: Substitute pork chops, tenderloin, or steak for lamb.

Lamb Chops in Foil

 1 lamb chop

¼ small eggplant, unpeeled, sliced

¼ large onion, sliced

½ small tomato, quartered

½ small green pepper, sliced

   Dash dried basil

   Salt or salt substitute

   Pepper

   Dash garlic salt or curry powder

Place lamb chop on piece of aluminum foil large enough to make roomy envelope for all ingredients.

Place remaining ingredients on top of lamb chop in order listed. Seal foil tightly to assure no steam escaping. Place on baking sheet or pan.

Bake in oven preheated to 350°F. for 1¼ hours.

1 serving.

Leftover Lamb Curry

Good enough for party fare.

2 tablespoons butter or margarine

1 large celery stalk, chopped

1 small onion, chopped

1 small apple, peeled, cored, and diced

1 tablespoon flour

1 cup leftover diced roast lamb

1 cup consommé or Bouillon (p. 27), or
    1 teaspoon instant beef- or chicken-
    flavored bouillon dissolved in 1 cup water,
    or 1 cup milk mixed with 1 teaspoon
    bottled brown bouquet sauce

½ teaspoon salt or salt substitute

⅛ teaspoon pepper

½ to 1 teaspoon curry (depending on
    personal taste for intensity of flavor)

2 teaspoons lemon juice

Melt butter in 3-cup saucepan and add celery, onion, and apple. Cook until onion is soft. Add flour, stirring well; then add lamb. Stir in consommé; then add remaining ingredients. Cook over low heat for at least 30 minutes. Serve over cooked rice.

2 to 3 servings.

Lamb and Eggplant Casserole

2 to 3 lamb shoulder steaks

1 teaspoon salt or salt substitute

¼ teaspoon pepper

⅛ teaspoon ground cinnamon

¾ cup thinly sliced onion

1 small eggplant, peeled and diced

2 tablespoons butter or margarine

½ cup water

8-ounce can tomato sauce

1 cup frozen, canned, or fresh peas

Place lamb on aluminum foil in shallow pan and score edges with knife.

Broil, turning once, until lightly browned. Trim off fat and bone; cut into bite-size pieces. Place in 1-quart casserole with cover; then mix meat with salt, pepper, cinnamon, and onion.

Cook eggplant in butter in 3-cup saucepan, stirring frequently. When tender, add water, tomato sauce, and peas. Mix well; then add to meat and stir until blended. Cover.

Bake at 325°F. for 1½ to 2 hours.

2 to 3 servings.

Lamb Loaf

Leftover lamb loaf makes good stuffed peppers.

1 pound ground lamb

⅓ cup dry bread crumbs

1 beaten egg

⅓ cup milk or skim, 2% fat or reconstituted
instant dry milk

1 teaspoon salt or salt substitute

¼ teaspoon ground pepper

⅛ teaspoon garlic powder

⅓ cup minced onion

1 tablespoon soy sauce

1 teaspoon prepared mustard

Combine all ingredients in 1-quart mixing bowl. Shape
into loaf and place in 7½ x 3½ x 2-inch loaf pan.
  Bake at 350°F. for about 40 minutes.
  2 to 3 servings.

Lamb with Mushrooms

1½ pounds lamb shoulder steak, trimmed
         and cubed
  1 small onion, chopped
  1 small clove garlic, minced
  ½ cup chopped celery
  1 cup water
  1 teaspoon salt or salt substitute
  ½ teaspoon paprika
  ¼ teaspoon caraway seed or ⅛ teaspoon
         ground cloves
  2 teaspoons prepared horseradish
  ¼ teaspoon pepper
     2-ounce can mushrooms or ½ cup fresh,
         sliced mushrooms
  1 tablespoon cornstarch
     Cooked rice

Place cubed meat in 1-quart casserole with cover. Add
onion, garlic, celery, water, salt, paprika, caraway seed,
horseradish and pepper; then mix well. Cover.

Bake at 325°F. for 2 hours, or until meat is tender;
then add mushrooms and cook 30 minutes longer. Remove from oven to stove top.

Mix cornstarch with a little cold water and stir into
meat mixture. Cook over medium-low heat, stirring
continually, until mixture is thickened. Serve over
rice. **2 servings.**

Creole Lamb Shanks

2 lamb shanks, trimmed of fat and cartilage

1 tablespoon olive oil (optional)

1 small clove garlic, minced

1 small green pepper, diced

Juice of ½ lemon (optional)

1 teaspoon salt or salt substitute

¼ teaspoon pepper

¼ teaspoon dried rosemary

8-ounce can tomato sauce

¼ cup water

Place lamb on aluminum foil in shallow pan and broil, turning once, until lightly browned.

Arrange lamb shanks in casserole with cover that best accommodates their size and shape.

Combine remaining ingredients in 2-cup bowl; then pour over lamb shanks. Cover.

Bake at 325°F. for 2½ hours, or until meat is very tender.

2 servings.

Hawaiian Lamb Shanks

2 lamb shanks, trimmed of fat and cartilage

1 teaspoon prepared mustard

1 teaspoon instant beef-flavored bouillon or
      1 cube instant beef bouillon, or 1 cup
      consommé, beef bouillon, or Beef Bouillon
      (p. 27)

3 tablespoons soy sauce or 2 teaspoons diet
      Worcestershire sauce

1 small clove garlic, minced

2 tablespoons apple-mint jelly, honey, or
      brown sugar

¾ cup hot water (if using instant bouillon)

Arrange lamb shanks in casserole with cover that best
accommodates their size and shape.

Combine remaining ingredients in small bowl or
cup; then pour over lamb shanks. Cover.

Bake at 325°F. for 2½ hours, or until meat is very
tender.

2 servings.

Lamb Shanks with Rice

2 lamb shanks, trimmed of fat and cartilage

Salt or salt substitute

Pepper

Garlic salt

½ cup uncooked rice

1-serving envelope onion soup mix
  1 cup Onion Soup (p. 30)

1½ cups water (if using soup mix)

Arrange shanks in casserole with cover that best accommodates their size and shape. Sprinkle with salt, pepper, and liberally with garlic salt.

Bake, uncovered, at 350°F. for one hour; then add rice, soup, and water, brushing rice off top of lamb. Cover.

Bake for another hour, or until meat is tender and rice is desired doneness.

2 servings.

Irish Lamb Stew

In Erin they don't believe in carrots, turnips, or barley in their stew. Leftover leg of lamb is used in this recipe.

Fat-free lamb drippings if any are left over from
     roasting leg of lamb or 1 tablespoon
     cooking oil
 1 medium potato, sliced
 1 cup cut-up or sliced leftover lamb
 1 medium onion, sliced
    Dried thyme
    Dried parsley
    Salt or salt substitute
    Pepper
½ cup water

Spread any drippings left from cooking lamb or cooking oil in bottom of 1-quart casserole with cover. Arrange a layer of potato slices in casserole; sprinkle very lightly with thyme, parsley, salt, and pepper. Place a layer of meat on top and sprinkle again with seasonings. Top with layer of onions, sprinkle with seasonings; then repeat three layers once more. Pour water over all and cover.

Bake at 325°F. for about 1½ hours, or until vegetables are tender.

2 servings.

PORK

Canadian-Style Bacon in Sauce

Canadian-style bacon is an all-around performer!
Serve as entreé or use in place of bacon or ham to add
oomph to vegetable cookery and in casseroles.

4 slices Canadian-style bacon, ¼-inch thick

¼ cup catsup or diet catsup

¼ teaspoon salt or salt substitute

¼ teaspoon celery salt or seed

Dash ground nutmeg

2 teaspoons lemon juice

Arrange Canadian-style bacon slices in shallow baking
dish lined with aluminum foil.

Mix remaining ingredients together in small bowl or
cup; then spread over bacon.

Bake at 325°F. for 30 minutes.

2 servings.

ALTERNATE I: See Leftover Ham Slices in Sauce
(p. 108). Substitute Canadian-style bacon for ham.

ALTERNATE II: See Glazed Ham Steak (p. 109). Substitute Canadian-style bacon for ham.

Hawaiian Ham Casserole

⅓ cup uncooked macaroni

1½ cups boiling water

½ teaspoon salt or salt substitute

½ cup diced cooked ham

¼ cup pineapple chunks or calorie-reduced
pineapple tidbits, drained

¼ cup chopped nuts or water chestnuts (try
macadamias for a wonderful surprise)

2 teaspoons margarine or butter

2 teaspoons flour

⅔ cup milk or skim, 2% fat or reconstituted
instant dry milk

⅛ teaspoon ground ginger

1 teaspoon soy sauce or diet
Worcestershire sauce

¼ teaspoon prepared mustard

Few grains pepper

HAWAIIAN HAM CASSEROLE
— *Continued*

Cook macaroni in boiling water and salt in 3-cup stove-to-oven casserole; then drain. Add ham, pineapple, and nuts; mix well.

Mix margarine with flour in 1-cup saucepan; add milk, ginger, soy sauce, mustard, and pepper. Cook over medium heat until cream sauce is thickened; then add to ham mixture and blend thoroughly.

Bake at 350°F. for about 25 minutes.

2 servings.

ALTERNATE: For Hawaiian Ham and Sweet Potato Casserole: Substitute ⅔ cup cooked, mashed sweet potatoes for cooked macaroni and add 1 tablespoon chopped green pepper, if desired.

Ham Loaf

Leftover ham loaf makes marvelous stuffed peppers, casseroles, and sandwiches. Try it teamed with hard-cooked eggs; then creamed and served over toast or English muffin.

1   beaten egg, ¼ cup frozen egg substitute or 2 tablespoons powdered egg substitute mixed with 2½ tablespoons water

¼   teaspoon salt or salt substitute

⅛   teaspoon pepper

2   teaspoons prepared horseradish

⅛   teaspoon dry mustard

1   green onion, minced

¼   cup saltine cracker crumbs or salt-free cracker crumbs

½   cup tomato sauce or Tomato Soup (p. 34), or 1-serving envelope cream of tomato soup mixed with ½ cup water

¾-pound ground, cooked ham

¼-pound ground, lean pork

HAM LOAF — *Continued*

Mix together egg, salt, pepper, horseradish, mustard, onion, crackers, and sauce or soup in 1-quart bowl. Add ham and pork; mix very well.

Form into loaf and place in shallow baking pan lined with aluminum foil or put into 6⅛ x 4¾ x 2-inch foil loaf pan.

Bake at 350°F. for about 45 minutes. Serve with sour cream mixed with applesauce or horseradish, if desired.

About 3 servings.

Leftover Ham Slices in Sauce

Enough leftover ham slices for one serving

2 tablespoons honey

1 tablespoon sherry

Dash ground cloves

1 or 2 apple slices, peeled and chopped

1 teaspoon minced onion

Arrange ham slices in 2-cup casserole or baking dish.
   Combine remaining ingredients in small bowl or
cup; then pour over ham.
   Bake in oven preheated to 350°F. for about 30 min.
1 serving.

ALTERNATE: For Leftover Ham Slices with Jelly:
Substitute 1 tablespoon currant or other tart red jelly
and 1 tablespoon prepared mustard, mixed together,
for honey, sherry, cloves, apples, and onion.

Glazed Ham Steak

If you have a yen for ham . . . but not a whole chunk
. . . find a nice sized slice for two at your meat coun-
ter and give it a festive glaze.

¾-pound cooked ham steak

> 1 tablespoon brown sugar or brown sugar
>   replacement
>
> 1 teaspoon prepared mustard
>
>   Dash ground cloves
>
> 1 tablespoon currant or other tart jelly

8¾-ounce can sliced peaches or calorie-
    reduced peaches, drained (reserve
    2 tablespoons juice)

Arrange ham steak in baking dish that will best accommodate its size and shape.

Mix together brown sugar, mustard, cloves, jelly,
and peach juice in small bowl or cup; then spread
over ham steak.

Arrange peach slices on top of ham.

Bake in oven preheated to 350°F. for 30 minutes,
basting with pan juices every 10 minutes. **2 servings.**

ALTERNATE: For Burgundy Glazed Ham Steak: Substitute 2 tablespoons burgundy mixed with 2 tablespoons honey for brown sugar, mustard, jelly, and
peach juice.

Pork Chops or Cutlets in Cranberry Sauce

Cranberry sauce isn't just for holidays. Try it in the new small-size can.

1 to 1¼ pounds loin pork chops or cutlets, trimmed of fat

Salt or salt substitute

Pepper

Garlic salt (optional)

⅓ cup jellied cranberry sauce

1 tablespoon brown sugar or brown sugar replacement

¼ teaspoon dry mustard

1 tablespoon dry white wine, orange, apple, or pineapple juice

Arrange chops in bottom of shallow baking pan lined with aluminum foil. Sprinkle with salt, pepper, and garlic salt.

Broil, turning once, just until browned. Pour off fat.

Mix together cranberry sauce, brown sugar, mustard, and white wine or fruit juice in small bowl or cup. Pour over pork.

Bake at 350°F. for about 45 minutes, or until done.
2 servings.

Easy Baked Pork Chop

1 pork loin chop, ¾-inch thick

1 tablespoon sour cream or sour cream substitute

2 teaspoons brown sugar or brown sugar replacement

1 teaspoon chopped onion or ⅛ teaspoon onion salt

⅛ teaspoon salt or salt substitute

Few grains pepper

Place pork chop in baking dish with cover.

Mix together sour cream, brown sugar, onion, salt, and pepper in small bowl or cup; then spread over pork chop. Cover.

Bake at 350°F. for 45 minutes. Remove cover and bake until golden brown.

1 serving.

ALTERNATE: For Easy Baked Pork Chop II: Add ¼ teaspoon prepared mustard and ¼ teaspoon Worcestershire sauce or diet Worcestershire sauce to sour cream mixture; then top with tomato slice or peach halve.

Gourmet Pork Chops

A jar of currant jelly adds such a dimension to entreés, fruits, and desserts. A little goes a long way, too, so don't shy away if it seems a bit expensive.

2 center cut pork tenderloin chops, ¾-inch
    thick, trimmed of fat

   Salt or salt substitute

   Pepper

2 unpeeled apple slices, ⅜-inch thick

2 tablespoons currant or apple jelly

Arrange chops in bottom of shallow baking pan lined with aluminum foil. Sprinkle with salt and pepper.
   Broil on one side only just until browned; remove from heat and pour off fat.
   Place an apple slice on each chop and spoon jelly into center of apple.
   Bake at 350°F. for 45 minutes.
   2 servings.

ALTERNATE: Gourmet Pork Chops for One: Divide all ingredients in half.

Individual Pork Chop Dinner in Foil

All ready to freeze and a size that will tuck away neatly in a small freezing compartment. Should you assemble several for the proverbial rainy day?

1 extra-thick pork chop, ½- to ¾-inch thick, trimmed of fat
2 tablespoons cream of celery soup
　Salt or salt substitute
　Pepper
　Garlic salt
　Fines herbes or mixed herbs
1 small potato, quartered
1 carrot, quartered
1 zucchini, quartered (optional)

Arrange meat in center of 12-inch square piece of aluminum foil. Spread soup over surface; then sprinkle alternately with salt, pepper, garlic salt, and fines herbes.

Arrange potato, carrot, and zucchini on top of meat. Fold ends of foil to middle and seal; then tightly seal sides.

Bake at 350°F. for 45 minutes to 1 hour. **1 serving.**

ALTERNATE: For Pork Roast in Foil: Substitute 2- to 3-pound pork loin roast for chops. Increase celery soup to 10½-ounce can and vegetables to the numbers desired.

Country-Style Ribs in Ginger Sauce

Adventure from the ordinary to easy exotica with stuff from two bottles, one can, and a few stand-by seasoners.

½ cup catsup or diet catsup

¼ cup chili sauce or diet chili sauce

8-ounce can crushed unsweetened pineapple

1 small clove garlic, minced, or ⅛ teaspoon garlic powder

1½ tablespoons brown sugar or brown sugar replacement

¼ teaspoon ground ginger

½ teaspoon salt or salt substitute

⅛ teaspoon pepper

1½ pounds pork loin country-style ribs

COUNTRY-STYLE RIBS IN GINGER SAUCE — *Continued*

Mix all ingredients except pork ribs in 2-cup saucepan. Simmer 30 minutes over low heat.

Meanwhile, arrange ribs in a shallow baking pan lined with aluminum foil. Broil, turning once, until browned. Drain off fat.

Spoon sauce over ribs; then bake at 300°F. for 2 hours, or until meat is tender. Refrigerate or freeze any remaining sauce.

2 servings.

ALTERNATE: For Chicken in Chinese Ginger Sauce: Substitute two broiler-fryer halves for ribs.

Notes:

Southern Pork Roast in Sauce

Compose your own frozen TV dinners from the succulent remaining roast pork.

¼ cup catsup or diet catsup

½ cup water

   Few drops Tabasco

2 teaspoons butter or margarine

2 tablespoons finely chopped onion or
   2 teaspoons instant chopped onion

¼ teaspoon salt or salt substitute

¼ teaspoon chili powder

¼ teaspoon celery seed or celery salt
   (optional)

1 tablespoon brown sugar or brown sugar
   replacement

1 tablespoon vinegar

1 tablespoon Worcestershire sauce or diet
   Worcestershire sauce

2- to 3-pound pork roast

SOUTHERN PORK ROAST IN SAUCE
— *Continued*

Mix all ingredients except pork roast in 2-cup sauce-pan and bring to boil.

Arrange pork roast in shallow baking pan lined with aluminum foil. Spoon half of sauce over meat.

Bake at 325°F. for about 2½ hours, spooning additional sauce over roast during baking.

About 4 servings, depending on size of roast.

ALTERNATE: For Pork Chops in Sauce: Substitute pork chops for roast, using any number up to eight. If one or a few chops is all that is needed, remaining sauce may be refrigerated or frozen.

Notes:

Teriyaki Pork

1 to 1½ pounds thinly sliced pork cutlet, tenderloin, or chops

2 tablespoons soy sauce or 1 teaspoon diet Worcestershire sauce

1 teaspoon sugar or sugar replacement

¼ teaspoon ground ginger

¼ teaspoon pepper or lemon pepper

1 teaspoon instant chopped onion or ⅛ teaspoon garlic powder

2 tablespoons dry red wine (optional)

4¾-ounce jar baby food peach cobbler

Arrange pork in bottom of shallow baking dish lined with aluminum foil.

Mix together remaining ingredients in small bowl or cup; then pour over pork. Marinate for a few hours or overnight in refrigerator.

Bake in oven preheated to 350°F. for about 45 minutes, or until meat is tender, or broil, turning once and basting occasionally with marinade until desired doneness.

2 servings.

VEAL

Veal Cutlet or Patties with Mushrooms

1 teaspoon cooking oil

¾-pound thinly sliced veal cutlet or
    chopped veal steaks

¼ cup water

¼ cup dry white wine or 2 teaspoons
    lemon juice

¼ teaspoon garlic salt or dash garlic powder

⅛ teaspoon dried rosemary

¼ teaspoon salt or salt substitute

⅛ teaspoon pepper

2-ounce can mushroom stems and pieces
    with liquid

Lightly coat with cooking oil a 9-inch skillet or pan with cover. Quickly brown veal over medium-high heat. Remove meat and add water, mixing and loosening pan drippings. Add wine, garlic salt, rosemary, salt, pepper, mushrooms, and liquid; then lower heat. Arrange veal in sauce, cover and simmer for 15 to 20 minutes.

2 servings.

Italian Veal Roast or Shanks

Choose a larger size roast or four shanks, if you would like a second meal of truly outstanding stew. Increase the vegetables accordingly, too.

2½ to 4 pounds veal rump, round, or loin
        roast, or 2 to 4 veal shanks

  2 tablespoons olive or cooking oil
        (olive is best)

½ cup chopped carrots

½ cup chopped celery

¼ cup chopped onion or 2 green onions,
        cut-up

⅓ cup dry white wine

  1-inch piece lemon peel

¼ teaspoon dried basil

½ teaspoon dried parsley

¼ teaspoon dried thyme

  1 teaspoon salt or salt substitute

¼ teaspoon pepper

  2 teaspoons flour

ITALIAN VEAL ROAST OR SHANKS
— Continued

½ cup water

1 potato per serving, peeled

1 carrot per serving, peeled

Place meat in 2-quart casserole with cover.

Mix together olive or cooking oil, chopped carrots, celery, onions, wine, lemon peel, basil, parsley, thyme, salt, and pepper in 2-cup bowl.

Mix together flour and water in small bowl or cup. Add to vegetable mixture; then pour over meat. Cover.

Bake at 325°F. for 2 to 2½ hours, or until meat is tender.

Notes:

Veal Stew

1 pound boneless veal cut into 1-inch cubes

1 tablespoon cooking oil

8½-ounce can small, whole onions with liquid

½ cup chopped celery

1-serving envelope cream of mushroom
      soup mixed with ¾ cup water or ¾ cup
      canned cream of mushroom soup

1 teaspoon chicken-flavored instant bouillon

1 cup water

3 tablespoons uncooked rice

1 teaspoon Worcestershire sauce or diet
      Worcestershire sauce

½ cup frozen or canned peas

Brown meat in oil in 2-quart casserole with cover. Add remaining ingredients except peas and cover.

Bake in oven preheated to 350°F. for 1½ hours. Stir; then add peas. Cover and return to oven for about 20 minutes.

2 to 3 servings.

Wienerschnitzel

Although veal has become expensive and hard to find, don't be denied the subtle treasure of flavors that it brings to your table. The chopped veal steaks are a reliable and less costly substitute.

1 tablespoon butter or margarine

1 tablespoon cooking oil

¾ pound chopped veal steaks

   Flour

   Salt or salt substitute

   Pepper

1 tablespoon finely minced onion

1 tomato, cut up

2 tablespoons sour cream or sour cream substitute

⅛ teaspoon paprika

Continued on following page

WIENERSCHNITZEL — *Continued*

Heat butter and oil in 9-inch skillet with cover.

Dredge meat in flour; then cook in butter and oil until browned, turning once. Sprinkle with salt and pepper and remove from skillet to plate.

Add onion to drippings and cook until soft; then add tomato and mix well, quickly scraping drippings from pan bottom into tomatoes and onions. Place meat on top and cover.

Bake at 325°F. for 20 minutes; then remove meat to piece of aluminum foil and keep warm in very low oven.

Stir sour cream and paprika into same skillet with drippings; then add more salt, if needed. Return meat to sauce and heat just until warmed through; do not boil.

2 servings.

Notes:

Poultry

• Barbequed Chicken for Two

Another recipe that is easily increased if you are having company.

2 large chicken breasts, 4 chicken thighs or legs, or ½ broiler-fryer

¼ cup bottled barbecue sauce

2 tablespoons frozen concentrated orange juice

Arrange chicken in 7- or 8-inch baking dish lined with aluminum foil.

Mix together barbecue sauce and orange juice in small bowl or cup. Spoon over chicken.

Bake at 350°F. for 1 hour, or until tender, depending on size of chicken pieces.

2 servings.

Bombay Chicken and Avocado

    1 tablespoon butter or margarine
  1/3 cup chopped onion
  1/3 cup peeled and chopped apple
  1/2 cup cream of chicken soup
  1/4 teaspoon salt or salt substitute
       Few grains pepper
  1/4 teaspoon curry powder (more, if desired)
    1 cup cooked, diced chicken
1 1/2 cups cooked rice
    1 avocado, peeled, halved, and seed
       removed

Melt butter in 3-cup saucepan; then add onion and apple and cook until onion is soft. Add chicken soup, salt, pepper, and curry powder and continue to cook until smooth, stirring continually. Add chicken; mix gently, but well.

Place rice in greased 7-inch square baking dish (or equivalent) and arrange peeled avocado halves on top. Fill center of avocado with chicken mixture.

Bake at 325°F. for about 15 minutes. **2 servings.**

ALTERNATE I: For Bombay Turkey and Avocado: Substitute turkey for chicken.

ALTERNATE II: For Bombay Shrimp and Avocado: Substitute cooked, deveined, and cut-up shrimp for chicken.

Quick Chicken or Turkey Casserole

2 cups cooked, diced chicken or turkey

1 cup small pieces fresh white bread

½ cup cooked rice

2 tablespoons chopped pimiento

½ teaspoon salt

2 beaten eggs, ½ cup frozen egg substitute, or 4 tablespoons (1 envelope) powdered egg substitute mixed with 5 tablespoons water

2 tablespoons butter or margarine

1 cup milk or skim, 2% fat or reconstituted instant dry milk

⅛ teaspoon pepper

⅔ cup cream of mushroom soup or 1-serving envelope cream of mushroom soup mixed with ⅔ cup water

1 tablespoon sherry (optional)

Continued on following page

QUICK CHICKEN OR TURKEY CASSEROLE — *Continued*

Combine all ingredients except mushroom soup and sherry in 1-quart mixing bowl. Pour into generously greased 1-quart casserole.

Bake in oven preheated to 325°F. for 1¼ hours.

Heat mushroom soup and sherry in 1-cup saucepan. Spoon over each serving of chicken.

3 to 4 servings.

Notes:

•Leftover Chicken Casserole

This dish gets better and better with each optional ingredient added.

1 cup cut-up cooked chicken

⅔ cup cream of celery, chicken, or
    mushroom soup

1 hard-cooked egg, chopped (optional)

¼ teaspoon curry powder or seasoned salt
    (optional)

2-ounce can mushroom stems and pieces,
    drained

1 cup cooked noodles or rice

1 tablespoon sherry or dry white wine
    (optional)

2 tablespoons chopped green pepper or
    1 teaspoon dried sweet pepper

¼ cup bread, cereal, or potato chip crumbs

Combine all ingredients except crumbs in 3-cup mixing bowl. Pour into greased 3-cup casserole and sprinkle crumbs over top.

    Bake at 325°F. for 25 to 30 minutes. **2 servings.**

ALTERNATE: For Leftover Turkey Casserole: Substitute turkey for chicken.

Chicken or Turkey Chow Mein

One doctor and authority on arthritis thinks simple Chinese cooking such as this reliable dish is therapeutic for arthritics.

1-pound can chow mein vegetables with
     liquid

2-ounce can mushroom stems and pieces
     with liquid

1 teaspoon or 1 cube instant chicken-
     flavored bouillon

Water

1½ tablespoons cornstarch

2 teaspoons sugar or sugar substitute

2 tablespoons soy sauce

1 green onion and tops, chopped, or
     2 teaspoons instant chopped onion

1 cup diced, cooked chicken

3-ounce can chow mein noodles or
     1½ cups cooked rice

CHICKEN OR TURKEY CHOW MEIN
— *Continued*

Drain liquid from vegetables and mushroom pieces into measuring cup; then add water to make 1 cup. Add chicken bouillon.

Mix a little vegetable liquid with cornstarch; then return to liquid and mix well. Pour into 3-cup saucepan; then add sugar, soy sauce, and green onions. Cook over medium heat, stirring continually, until thickened. Add chow mein vegetables, mushrooms and chicken; cook until bubbling hot.

Serve chow mein mixture over heated chow mein noodles or rice.

2 servings.

ALTERNATE: For Leftover Pork Chow Mein: Substitute leftover, cooked pork for chicken.

Notes:

● **Chicken or Turkey Divan**

. . . . for one, two, three, four, and more, if you wish.

- 2 thawed frozen broccoli spears or 2 fresh broccoli spears, cooked just until tender

- 2 teaspoons margarine or butter

- 2 teaspoons flour

- ½ cup milk or skim, 2% fat or reconstituted milk or half and half cream or non-dairy, polyunsaturated creamer

- ¼ teaspoon salt or salt substitute

  Few grains pepper

  Few grains ground nutmeg

  Dash Worcestershire sauce or diet Worcestershire sauce

- 1 tablespoon mayonnaise or diet mayonnaise (optional)

- 1 tablespoon sherry or dry white wine (optional, but very good)

- 2 to 3 slices cooked turkey or chicken, packaged turkey slices, or equivalent thawed frozen diced chicken

  Parmesan cheese

CHICKEN OR TURKEY DIVAN
— *Continued*

Arrange broccoli in small shallow casserole to accommodate it's length or, if necessary, cut broccoli spears in half and arrange in casserole.

Melt margarine in 1-cup saucepan;then stir in flour. Add milk, salt, pepper, nutmeg, Worcestershire sauce, and mayonnaise. Cook over medium-low heat, stirring continually, until thickened. Add wine; mix well.

Pour half of sauce over broccoli and sprinkle with Parmesan cheese. Arrange chicken or turkey slices on top of cheese; then pour on remaining sauce and sprinkle with Parmesan cheese.

Bake at 325°F. for about 35 minutes or until bubbling hot.

1 serving.

Notes:

Gourmet Chicken

Five stars for this easily increased, uniquely flavored formula.

2 to 3 chicken pieces of choice

   Salt

   Pepper

1 tablespoon apricot preserves

1 tablespoon Russian salad dressing or Old-
   Fashioned Dressing (p. 176)

Place sheet of aluminum foil in bottom of shallow baking dish.

Wash and dry chicken; arrange on aluminum foil skin-side-up. Sprinkle with salt and pepper.

Mix together apricot preserves and salad dressing in cup or small bowl; then pour over chicken.

Bake at 350°F. for 1¼ to 1½ hours, basting occasionally.

1 serving.

Hawaiian Chicken

2 to 4 chicken breasts, ½ broiler-fryer, or
    4 chicken thighs

¼ cup soy sauce

    Juice of ½ lemon or lime or 2 tablespoons
    white wine

⅛ teaspoon pepper or seasoned pepper

⅛ teaspoon garlic powder

⅛ teaspoon ground ginger (optional)

Arrange chicken in shallow baking pan lined with aluminum foil.

Mix together remaining ingredients in small bowl or cup. Pour over chicken.

Broil on rack farthest from broiler element or flame for about 30 minutes, or until well browned. Turn, skin-side-up, and broil until well browned, basting occasionally with marinade.

Reduce oven to 350°F. and bake about 15 minutes, or until marinade has thickened.

2 servings.

Chicken Paprika

For an effortless dividend, cook some extra chicken in this flavorful manner. It makes unusually good creamed chicken or chicken salad.

¼ cup finely chopped onion

¼ cup finely chopped green pepper

¼ cup finely chopped celery (optional)

 1 tablespoon cooking oil or margarine

½ cup cut-up tomatoes, peeled and seeds
    removed

½ cup water

1 teaspoon instant chicken-flavored bouillon,
    1 chicken bouillon cube, or 1-serving
    envelope instant chicken-flavored broth

½ teaspoon paprika

¾ teaspoon salt or salt substitute

 2 to 4 chicken breasts, ½ broiler-fryer, or
    4 chicken thighs

1½ tablespoons flour

⅓ cup sour cream or sour cream substitute

CHICKEN PAPRIKA — *Continued*

Cook onion and green pepper in oil in 2-quart casserole with cover. When vegetables are soft, add tomatoes, water, bouillon, paprika, and salt; mix very well.

Arrange chicken in casserole, spoon sauce over chicken pieces and cover.

Bake at 325°F. for 30 minutes. Remove from oven.

Pour liquid off chicken into measuring cup. Skim off fat and measure ⅓ cup liquid and pour into 1-cup saucepan. Save remaining broth for cooking another time. Keep chicken warm while finishing sauce.

Mix flour with sour cream and add to liquid in saucepan. Cook, stirring continually, until thickened, but do not boil.

Pour sauce over chicken, cover and bake 30 to 40 minutes longer.

2 or more servings, depending on number of chicken pieces.

Notes:

Chicken in Sour Cream

Cook the larger number of pieces because another day you can debone and dice leftover chicken, skim off fat from pan gravy, heat together and serve over toast.

2 to 4 chicken breasts or 4 to 6 chicken thighs

5 tablespoons sour cream or sour cream substitute

1½ tablespoons lemon juice

2 teaspoons Worcestershire sauce or diet Worcestershire sauce

Dash garlic powder or garlic salt

⅛ teaspoon paprika

⅛ teaspoon pepper

¼ cup fresh bread crumbs (optional)

Arrange chicken, skin-side-up, in 8-inch square baking dish.

Mix together sour cream and remaining ingredients, except bread crumbs, in small bowl or cup. Spread over each chicken piece. Marinate 1 hour to overnight in refrigerator.

Bake at 350°F. for 1¼ to 1½ hours. Sprinkle bread crumbs over chicken for last 30 minutes of baking.

2 to 4 servings, depending on number of chicken pieces.

Rock Cornish Game Hen

1 or 2 Rock Cornish game hens, 1 pound each

¼ cup dry white or rosé wine

¼ cup brown sugar or brown sugar replacement

½ teaspoon salt

1 tablespoon cider vinegar

1-serving envelope instant onion soup
    or ½ cup Onion Soup (p. 30)

Dash ground cloves

Wash and dry birds. Cut them in half, if you wish to use one bird for two servings. Arrange in bottom of baking dish lined with aluminum foil.

Mix together remaining ingredients in small bowl or cup. Spoon 2 to 3 spoonfuls of sauce over birds.

Bake in oven preheated to 350°F. for 1¼ hours, basting every 20 minutes with additional sauce. Birds may be arranged breast-side-down at beginning of baking and turned up after 45 minutes, if desired.

2 servings.

Brunswick Stew

If you are on a low-ruffage diet, but hate to miss the sweet corn season, run a sharp knife down each row of corn kernels, allowing the meat to escape the skin and making it safe to eat.

3-pound broiler-fryer, cut-up
1 small onion, sliced
½ cup okra (optional)
1 cup fresh or canned tomatoes
1 cup frozen lima beans
1 potato, sliced
1 cup fresh or canned corn
1 teaspoon salt or salt substitute
¼ teaspoon pepper
2 teaspoons sugar or granulated sugar
    replacement

Simmer chicken in water to cover in 2-quart saucepan with cover for 2 hours, or until meat is tender and easily removed from bones. Remove chicken.

Add remaining ingredients to chicken broth and simmer, uncovered, about 40 minutes, or until vegetables are tender.

Bone and cut up chicken. Add to cooked vegetables. Cook until liquid is reduced, stirring occasionally to prevent scorching.

4 servings.

Method for Roasting Turkey Breast or Thigh

A beautiful beginning for many good things made from cooked turkey. Be sure and save the pan juices too.

2½-pound (about) half of turkey breast or
     equivalent in thigh meat

    Salt or salt substitute

    Pepper

    Garlic salt with parsley, garlic salt, or
       garlic powder

2 stalks celery

Place a 24-inch sheet of aluminum foil across shallow baking pan.

Wash turkey; cut off any excess skin or fat and sprinkle skin side liberally with salt and pepper. Place bone-side-up (cavity) on aluminum foil. Sprinkle liberally with salt, pepper, and garlic; then place celery across top. Bring ends of aluminum foil together and seal; then tightly seal sides.

Bake at 300°F. for 2¼ hours or until tender, depending upon size of turkey piece.

Remove from oven and leave sealed in aluminum foil until cooled, as this makes the meat very moist.

Salads

Avocado Ring

This will put a ring around your best chicken, seafood, or vegetable salad mixtures. Or why not a surprise fruit combination that includes papaya or melon?

1 envelope (1 tablespoon) unflavored gelatin

⅓ cup cold water

1 cup mashed avocado (about 1 medium)

1 cup buttermilk

¼ cup mayonnaise or diet mayonnaise

⅛ teaspoon celery salt

⅛ teaspoon onion salt

2 teaspoons lemon juice

Few grains pepper

Few drops Tabasco

Sprinkle gelatin over cold water in 3-cup saucepan. Heat over low heat until gelatin is dissolved. Remove from stove and add remaining ingredients. Pour into 3-cup mold and refrigerate until firm.

4 servings.

Unique Beet Salad

- 1 cup cooked diced beets
- ¼ cup very thinly sliced onions
- ⅓ cup diced unpeeled or peeled apples
- 2 tablespoons chopped dill pickle or ¼ teaspoon dried dill weed
- 2 tablespoons mayonnaise or diet mayonnaise
- 1½ teaspoons vinegar

  Lettuce leaves

Combine beets, onions, apples, and pickles in 2-cup bowl.

Mix together mayonnaise and vinegar. Blend with beet mixture. Serve on lettuce leaf.

2 servings.

•Carrots Vinaigrette

8¾-ounce can tiny whole carrots or 1 cup
    cooked fresh or frozen carrots

1½ tablespoons cooking oil

 2 teaspoons lemon juice

 ¼ teaspoon fines herbes or mixed herbs

   Lettuce leaves

Combine all ingredients in 2-cup bowl. Refrigerate at least 2 hours, stirring occasionally. Serve carrots on lettuce leaf; then spoon remaining marinade over top of carrots.
   2 servings.

ALTERNATE: For Quick Carrots Vinaigrette: Substitute 2 tablespoons bottled Italian dressing for oil, lemon juice, and herbs.

Versatile Molded Fruit Salad

Write your own ticket by choosing favored gelatin flavor and favorite fruits.

> 3-ounce package fruit-flavored gelatin or 4-serving envelope low-calorie, low-sodium fruit-flavored gelatin dessert
>
> 1½ cups lemon-lime carbonated beverage or low-calorie carbonated beverage
>
> 8-ounce can unsweetened, crushed pineapple and juice
>
> 1 small banana, cut-up (optional)
>
> ½ cup whipped cottage cheese or low-fat cottage cheese (optional)

Dissolve gelatin in carbonated beverage in 1-quart saucepan over low heat; refrigerate until consistency of unbeaten egg white.

Fold in fruit and whipped cottage cheese. Pour into mold, dish, individual plastic glasses or waxed cups; refrigerate until firm.

Makes 4 servings.

VERSATILE MOLDED FRUIT SALAD
— *Continued*

ALTERNATE I: Substitute syrup from canned fruits or fruit juice for carbonated beverage.

ALTERNATE II: Substitute up to 2 cups of any fruit except fresh pineapple for crushed pineapple and banana.

ALTERNATE III: Substitute whipped cream or whipped low-calorie dessert topping, sour cream, or sour cream substitute for cottage cheese.

ALTERNATE IV: To make one-half recipe (2 servings), substitute 3 tablespoons fruit gelatin for 3-ounce package; reduce carbonated beverage, fruit, and cottage cheese to half.

Notes:

Molded Gazpacho Salad

This queen of aspics allows you the latitude of using what you like or what you have on hand as long as it is 1 cup liquid and 1 cup vegetables.

1½ teaspoons unflavored gelatin

1 teaspoon sugar or granulated sugar replacement

1 cup vegetable juice cocktail, tomato juice, or tomato juice with herbs or spices

Few drops Tabasco

2 teaspoons cider vinegar or wine vinegar

¼ teaspoon salt or salt substitute

Few grains pepper

¼ teaspoon Worcestershire sauce or diet Worcestershire sauce (optional)

Dash garlic powder (optional)

⅓ cup finely chopped tomato, peeled and seeds removed, if desired

MOLDED GAZPACHO SALAD—*Continued*

⅓ cup finely chopped cucumber, peeled
and seeds removed, if desired

2 tablespoons finely chopped green pepper

1 tablespoon finely chopped green onion

½ teaspoon freeze dried chives (optional)

Mix gelatin with sugar in 2-cup saucepan; then add ½ cup vegetable juice. Stir over low heat until gelatin is dissolved. Remove from heat and add remaining vegetable juice, Tabasco, vinegar, salt, pepper, Worcestershire sauce and garlic powder, stirring to blend. Refrigerate until consistency of unbeaten egg white.

Fold in remaining ingredients and pour into 2-cup mold.

2 to 3 servings.

Changeable Gelatin Salad

Who is to say what you should put in your molded fruit or vegetable salad. This recipe will head you in the right direction as to making fewer servings, but won't inhibit your imagination or personal prefer-. ences.

3 tablespoons or one-half 3-ounce package fruit- or citrus-flavored gelatin of choice, or low-calorie, low-sodium gelatin dessert of choice

1 cup water, fruit juice, carbonated beverage, or low-calorie carbonated beverage

1 cup cottage cheese or low-fat cottage cheese (optional)

¼ cup mayonnaise or diet mayonnaise (optional)

½ to 1 cup canned or fresh fruit (except pineapple) or vegetables

¼ cup nutmeats, waterchestnuts, or toasted soy nuts (optional)

CHANGEABLE GELATIN SALAD
— *Continued*

Sprinkle gelatin over ¼ cup fruit juice or carbonated beverage.

Heat remaining ¾ cup liquid in 3-cup saucepan; then add gelatin and stir until dissolved. Remove from heat and refrigerate until gelatin is consistency of unbeaten egg white.

Add cottage cheese, mayonnaise, fruit or vegetables, and nuts. Pour into 3-cup mold or bowl. Refrigerate until firm.

2 to 3 servings.

ALTERNATE: For Changeable Gelatin Dessert: Substitute ¼ cup (one-half 2-ounce package) low-calorie dessert topping mix whipped with ¼ cup cold milk and ¼ teaspoon vanilla extract for cottage cheese and mayonnaise.

Notes:

Holiday Salad

1   envelope unflavored gelatin

1   cup plus 1 tablespoon sugar or granulated
    sugar replacement

½   cup water

3   oranges

¼   cup lemon juice

½   cup halved seedless green grapes

¼   cup chopped nuts or waterchestnuts

¼   cup light raisins

6   dates, cut up

6   maraschino cherries, quartered

    Whipped cream, low-calorie dessert
    topping, sour cream, or sour cream
    substitute

HOLIDAY SALAD — *Continued*

Combine gelatin with 1 tablespoon sugar in 2-cup saucepan; then add water. Stir over low heat until gelatin is dissolved; then set aside.

Peel oranges and cut into sections over 1-quart bowl to catch juice. Measure juice and add enough more to make approximately 1 cup. Add remaining sugar, lemon juice, and gelatin, stirring until sugar is dissolved; then refrigerate until consistency of unbeaten egg white.

Fold in orange sections, grapes, nuts, raisins, dates, and cherries. Pour into 4-cup greased mold. Refrigerate overnight and serve with whipped cream.

4 to 6 servings.

Notes:

Lemon Cheese Mold with Shrimp Topping

3-ounce package lemon gelatin or low-calorie,
low-sodium gelatin dessert

1 cup boiling water

½ teaspoon salt or salt substitute

½ teaspoon prepared horseradish

Juice of ½ lemon

¼ cup coffee cream or polyunsaturated
frozen non-dairy creamer

3-ounce package cream cheese or ⅓ cup
lowered-fat cream cheese

½ cup sliced ripe olives

½ cup chopped celery

½ cup whipping cream, whipped, or ¼ cup
low-calorie dessert topping whipped
with ¼ cup cold milk

Dissolve gelatin in boiling water in 1-quart mixing
bowl; then add salt, horseradish, and lemon juice.
Refrigerate until consistency of unbeaten egg white.

LEMON CHEESE MOLD WITH SHRIMP TOPPING — *Continued*

Add cream, cream cheese, olives, and celery; mix well. Gently fold in whipped cream. Pour into 4-cup mold that has been rinsed in cold water.

SHRIMP TOPPING

½ cup mayonnaise or diet mayonnaise

1 tablespoon lemon juice

2 teaspoons minced onion

2 tablespoons chopped pimiento

¾ cup cooked cut-up shrimp

Combine all ingredients in 2-cup mixing bowl. Serve over lemon cheese mold.

4 servings.

ALTERNATE: For Lemon Cheese Mold with Crabmeat Topping: Substitute crabmeat for shrimp.

Macaroni Salad

How many times has this versatile cook's friend saved the noonday lunch or the nighttime dinner? The foundation salad keeps very well, and you can use it as a beginning for an emergency meal as it takes to fish, meat, and more vegetables in an instant.

1½ cups boiling water

½ teaspoon salt or salt substitute

1 teaspoon cooking oil

¾ cup uncooked macaroni

2 tablespoons mayonnaise or diet mayonnaise

1 teaspoon vinegar

Few grains pepper

1 green onion and top, chopped

1 hard-cooked egg, chopped

2 tablespoons chopped celery (optional)

2 tablespoons chopped radishes (optional)

2 tablespoons green pepper, sliced olives stuffed with pimiento, or pimiento (optional)

MACARONI SALAD — *Continued*

Bring water to boil in 3-cup saucepan; then add salt, oil, and macaroni and cook, stirring occasionally, until macaroni is just tender. Drain and leave in pan to cool.

Mix together mayonnaise, vinegar, pepper, and onion; then blend well and fold in egg and options. Add to macaroni and mix gently, but thoroughly, adding more salt, if necessary.

2 to 3 servings.

ALTERNATE I: For Macaroni Salad with Meat: Add ¼ cup cooked diced ham, ham loaf, corned beef, bologna, frankfurters, Canadian bacon, or roast beef.

ALTERNATE II: For Macaroni Salad with Seafood: Add 3¾-ounce can of tuna, drained, or ⅓ cup salmon, cooked white fish, shrimp or crabmeat and 2 teaspoons lemon juice.

Notes:

Hot Potato Salad Casserole

Marvelous cold, too!

2 cups diced, hot, cooked potatoes
(2 medium potatoes)

2 tablespoons dry white wine or lemon juice

1 tablespoon cooking oil

2 teaspoons cider vinegar

¼ teaspoon seasoned salt or seasoned salt
substitute

¼ teaspoon dry mustard

⅛ teaspoon pepper

⅛ teaspoon dried dill weed

2 finely chopped green onions and tops

2 to 3 tablespoons sour cream or sour cream
substitute

2 tablespoons mayonnaise or diet
mayonnaise

Gently combine all except last two ingredients in 1-quart mixing bowl; then add sour cream and mayonnaise. Turn into 3-cup casserole.

Bake at 350°F. for about 30 minutes, or until thoroughly heated.

2 to 3 servings.

Leftover Roast Beef Salad or Sandwich Filling

A very imaginative caterer features this filling salad in box lunches.

1 cup very finely chopped, leftover beef roast

½ cup diced celery

1 green onion, minced

¼ to ½ cup diced cheddar, Swiss, Monterey Jack cheese, or 99% fat-free or low-moisture, part-skim cheese

¼ cup mayonnaise or diet mayonnaise

2 teaspoons sweet pickle relish or 1 small dill pickle, finely chopped

½ teaspoon prepared horseradish (optional)

2 tablespoons catsup or diet catsup

¼ teaspoon salt or salt substitute

Few grains pepper

Mix all ingredients together in 3-cup bowl. Serve on lettuce leaf or between bread slices.

2 servings.

Salmon Mousse

The sliced, hard-cooked egg and pimiento-stuffed olives will be equally as delicious mixed in the salad or left out to garnish with colorful edibles.

1½ teaspoons unflavored gelatin

1 tablespoon sugar or granulated sugar replacement

2 tablespoons water

½ teaspoon salt or salt substitute

½ teaspoon prepared mustard

2 tablespoons lemon juice

1 teaspoon minced green onion or onion

1 teaspoon prepared horseradish

1 beaten egg yolk, ⅛ cup frozen egg substitute or 1 tablespoon powdered egg mixed with 1¼ tablespoons water

7¾-ounce can salmon, flaked

1 hard-cooked egg, (optional)

¼ cup chopped celery or waterchestnuts

SALMON MOUSSE — *Continued*

¼ cup whipped cream or 2 tablespoons low-calorie dessert topping mix whipped with ¼ cup cold milk until stiff

2 tablespoons sliced olives stuffed with pimiento (optional)

Mix gelatin with sugar in 3-cup saucepan. Add water, salt, mustard, lemon juice, onion, horseradish, and egg yolk. Cook over medium-low heat until mixture is thickened. Remove from heat and cool. Add salmon; then fold in remaining ingredients. Pour into 2-cup mold. **2 servings.**

ALTERNATE I: For Tuna Mousse: Substitute 7¼-ounce can oil- or water-packed tuna, rinsed, drained, and flaked for salmon.

ALTERNATE II: For Crab, Lobster, or Shrimp Mousse: Substitute 1 cup cooked, cut-up crabmeat, lobster, or shrimp for salmon.

ALTERNATE III: For Chicken Mousse: Substitute 1 cup cooked, cut-up chicken for salmon, add a dash of curry powder, if desired, and omit horseradish.

ALTERNATE IV: For Ham Mousse: Substitute 1 cup cooked, cut-up ham or ham loaf for salmon, and chopped sweet pickle for olives. Add 2 tablespoons catsup or diet catsup.

Tuna Salad

7-ounce can oil- or water-packed tuna
½ cup chopped celery
 1 finely chopped green onion
½ teaspoon salt or salt substitute
⅛ teaspoon pepper
⅛ teaspoon garlic salt or dash garlic powder
 2 teaspoons lemon juice
⅓ to ½ cup mayonnaise or diet mayonnaise
 2 hard-cooked eggs (optional)

Rinse tuna in cold water, if desired; then drain and flake into 2-cup bowl. Add celery, onion, salt, pepper, garlic salt, lemon juice, and mayonnaise. Mix well; then gently fold in eggs. Serve on lettuce leaf or in tomato cup. **2 servings.**

ALTERNATE I: For Salmon Salad: Substitute 7¾-ounce can salmon for tuna.

ALTERNATE II: For Tuna Fish Salad Sandwich Spread: Finely mince the tuna, celery, onion, and egg. Makes 4 sandwiches.

ALTERNATE III: For Hot Open-Face Tuna Sandwiches: Toast 4 slices bread and divide tuna salad mixture among them. Grate ½ cup cheese or low-moisture, part skim cheese and sprinkle over tuna fish; then sprinkle with paprika. Broil until cheese is melted and lightly brown.
Makes 4 sandwiches.

Cooked Mixed Vegetable Salad

A great variety of vegetable mixes from which to choose will give those on a low-bulk diet a tasty alternative to raw salads. Try Oriental, Italian, or Florentine frozen mixed vegetables.

1 cup mixed vegetables of choice, cooked just until tender

¼ teaspoon salt or salt substitute

⅛ teaspoon pepper

⅛ teaspoon dried dill weed

Dash garlic powder

⅓ cup cottage cheese, low-fat cottage cheese, or yogurt

Lettuce leaf (optional)

Paprika (optional)

Combine all ingredients in 2-cup bowl. Serve on lettuce leaf and sprinkle with paprika.

2 servings.

Salad Dressings

Best Basic Salad Dressing

Cooking with herbs opens up a whole new world of tastes and subtle variations in staple menu items. The cost is little; the rewards great.

 1 tablespoon imitation bacon bits or 1 strip
    bacon, cooked and crumbled
½ teaspoon dried oregano
 1 teaspoon dried parsley or 1 tablespoon
    fresh, chopped parsley
½ teaspoon freeze-dried chopped chives
½ teaspoon salt or salt substitute
⅛ teaspoon pepper
 1 clove garlic, cut in half (optional)
 3 tablespoons apple cider vinegar or wine
    vinegar or lemon juice
½ cup cooking oil or ¼ cup cooking oil and
    ¼ cup olive oil

Measure vinegar in 1-cup measuring cup or ½-pint jar with lid; then add all ingredients except oil and mix very well. Add oil, mix well, and refrigerate.
    Makes 1 cup.

Easy Salad Dressing

1 envelope (0.6-ounce) Italian salad dressing
    mix

1 cup buttermilk

¼ cup mayonnaise or diet mayonnaise

Put all ingredients in 1-pint jar with lid and mix well.
Refrigerate several hours or overnight before using.
    Makes 1½ cups.

Favorite Salad Dressing

This dressing (with slight variations) is often what restaurants call their "house dressing."

- 1 teaspoon sugar or granulated sugar replacement
- ½ teaspoon dry mustard
- ¼ teaspoon pepper or equivalent of freshly ground pepper
- ½ teaspoon salt or salt substitute
- ¼ teaspoon paprika
- ⅛ teaspoon garlic powder or 1 small clove garlic, mashed (optional)
- 1 tablespoon freshly chopped chives, parsley, or tarragon or 1 teaspoon freeze-dried chives, parsley flakes, or dried tarragon
- 2 tablespoons cider vinegar or wine vinegar
- 4 tablespoons cooking or olive oil
- 2 teaspoons lemon juice (optional)

Combine all ingredients except oil in ½-pint jar with lid, mix well; then add oil. Refrigerate.
Makes ½ cup.

Old-Fashioned French Dressing

One of the easiest ways to save money is to make your own salad dressings. A short time spent in the kitchen will yield several kinds that will serve your needs for several weeks.

½ cup cooking oil

¼ cup cider vinegar or wine vinegar

2 tablespoons sugar or granulated sugar replacement

⅓ cup chili sauce or diet chili sauce or catsup or diet catsup

½ teaspoon salt or salt substitute

1 teaspoon paprika

Combine all ingredients in 2-cup bowl or 1-pint jar with lid. Refrigerate.
   Makes 1¼ cups.

Honey-Lime Dressing for Fruit Salad

½ cup mayonnaise or diet mayonnaise

¼ cup honey

½ cup whipping cream, whipped or ¼ cup low-calorie dessert topping mix whipped with ¼ cup cold milk

2 tablespoons lime juice

Combine all ingredients in 2-cup bowl or ½-pint jar with lid. Refrigerate.
Makes 1¼ cups.

ALTERNATE: Dressing for Fruit Salad: Substitute currant jelly or apricot preserves for honey.

Roquefort or Blue Cheese Dressing

¼ cup mayonnaise or diet mayonnaise

2 tablespoons sour cream or sour cream substitute

2 teaspoons lemon juice or vinegar

Dash garlic salt or powder

1 teaspoon freeze-dried chives (optional)

¼ cup crumbled Roquefort or blue cheese

Few drops Tabasco (optional)

Mix together mayonnaise, sour cream, lemon juice, garlic salt, and chives in 1½ cup bowl. Fold in cheese. **Makes 1 cup.**

Sour Cream Substitute I

This reliable stand-in for sour cream may be added to hot dishes at the last moment or it is very good mixed with herbs and used as a dressing for salads or mousse.

> 2 tablespoons milk or skim, 2% fat or reconstituted instant dry milk
>
> 1 tablespoon lemon juice
>
> 1 cup low-fat or creamed cottage cheese
>
> ¼ teaspoon salt or salt substitute

Place all ingredients in 2-cup bowl or blender and mix until smooth. Creamy cottage cheese may be put through sieve first to speed mixing.
   Makes 1¼ cups.

Sour Cream Substitute II

> 1 cup evaporated milk or whipping cream
>
> 1 tablespoon vinegar or buttermilk

Mix all ingredients together in 2-cup bowl or jar with lid. Refrigerate.
   Makes 1 cup.

Homemade Yogurt

Yogurt may be used wherever sour cream or a sour cream substitute is called for in bread, cakes, and cookie recipes or to replace cream or milk in stews, quiche, salad dressings, sauces, and custards. It is much lower in calories than sour cream or sour cream substitute and less expensive.

2 cups milk or skim or 2% fat milk

2 tablespoons instant dry milk

1 tablespoon commercial yogurt

Combine milk and instant dry milk in 3-cup saucepan. Bring just to boiling point over medium-low heat, stirring occasionally. Remove from heat and transfer to 3-cup refrigerator dish or jar with cover.

Blend a little milk with yogurt until mixture is smooth; then add to milk and set in warm place. When mixture is consistency of thick cream, refrigerate.

Makes about 2¼ cups.

Vegetables

•Quick Baked Beans

Use the can as a baking dish. Just remove 1 or 2 table-spoons of the liquid, add the other taste-giving ingredients and bake in the oven.

8-ounce can pork and beans

1 tablespoon brown sugar or brown sugar replacement

1 tablespoon molasses

¼ teaspoon prepared mustard

Combine all ingredients in 2-cup saucepan and cook over medium-low heat until warmed through; or combine all ingredients in 1½-cup baking dish and bake at 350°F. for 35 to 45 minutes.
1 to 2 servings.

ALTERNATE: For Quick Baked Beans and Frankfurters: Add one sliced frankfurter to beans.

•Deviled Carrots

Carrots are a most congenial vegetable. Their lovely color brings life to a meal that may be otherwise drab; they are compatible with most meat, fish, and poultry, and they will not violate most diets. Keep a glass jar, can, or package of frozen carrots on hand.

8¼-ounce can carrots, drained, or 1 cup cooked
    fresh or frozen carrots, drained

2 teaspoons butter or margarine

1 tablespoon honey, brown sugar, or brown
    sugar replacement

¼ teaspoon salt or salt substitute

    Few grains pepper

3 drops Tabasco

1 teaspoon vinegar or lemon juice

¼ teaspoon dried parsley (optional, but a
    beautiful touch)

Mix all ingredients together in 2-cup saucepan. Cook over medium-low heat, stirring frequently until heated through and flavors are well blended.
    2 servings.

ALTERNATE: For Curried Carrots: Add ⅛ to ¼ teaspoon curry powder.

Cauliflower au Gratin

Potatoes, asparagus, lima beans, broccoli, or cabbage would be equally as good as cauliflower.

1   tablespoon butter or margarine

1   tablespoon flour

    Salt or salt substitute

    Pepper

½   cup milk or skim, 2% fat or reconstituted instant dry milk

¼   cup grated sharp or 99% fat-free cheese

½   teaspoon dried parsley

¼   teaspoon instant chopped or 1 teaspoon minced onion

2   cups or 1 small head cauliflower, cooked, or 10-ounce package frozen cauliflower, thawed and drained

1   to 2 tablespoons bread or cereal flake crumbs

    Paprika (optional)

Continued on following page

CAULIFLOWER AU GRATIN — *Continued*

Blend butter and flour in 2-cup saucepan; then add milk and cook over low heat, stirring continually, until thickened. Add cheese, parsley, onion, salt, and pepper to taste. Cook until cheese is melted.

Pour a small amount of cheese sauce into buttered 3-cup casserole; then arrange a layer of cauliflower over sauce. Continue to alternate layers of sauce and cauliflower, ending with sauce. Sprinkle crumbs on top; then paprika.

Bake at 375°F. for 20 to 30 minutes.

2 to 3 servings.

All-Season Celery

    4 large, outside stalks celery, diagonally
         sliced

    2 tablespoons butter or margarine

    ¼ cup chopped pecans, almonds, or water
         chestnuts

    1 small clove garlic, minced

    1 small green onion, chopped

    ½ teaspoon instant chicken bouillon

    ¼ teaspoon salt or salt substitute

Cook celery in butter in 2-cup saucepan with cover.
Add remaining ingredients; then cover and cook just
until celery is tender.

   2 servings.

Scalloped Creamed Corn

Discover the surprisingly enlarged selection of vegetables that are packed in small cans and small diet-pack cans.

¼ cup saltine cracker crumbs or salt-free cracker crumbs

¼ cup milk or skim, 2% fat or reconstituted instant dry milk

8¾-ounce can or 1 cup cream-style corn

¼ teaspoon salt or salt substitute
     Few grains pepper

1 beaten egg, ¼ cup frozen egg substitute, or 2 tablespoons powdered egg substitute mixed with 2½ tablespoons water

1 teaspoon dried sweet pepper flakes or 1 tablespoon diced green pepper or green chili pepper

Mix together all ingredients in 3-cup mixing bowl. Pour into 2-cup casserole or baking dish.

Bake in oven preheated to 350°F. for 35 to 40 min. **2 servings.**

ALTERNATE: For one-dish meal, add ½ cup cooked diced ham, bologna, or Canadian bacon and top with ¼ cup shredded cheddar or 99% fat-free cheese.

Southern Eggplant Casserole

Don't be without Parmesan cheese. It adds impor-
tance to many soups, pastas, and casseroles.

1 small eggplant

Water

1 teaspoon salt or salt substitute

2 teaspoons cooking oil

¼ cup finely chopped onion

2 teaspoons dried sweet pepper flakes or
   2 tablespoons minced green pepper

Few grains pepper

1 to 2 tablespoons very fine fresh bread
   crumbs

1 slightly beaten egg, ¼ cup frozen egg
   substitute, or 2 tablespoons powdered
   egg substitute mixed with 2½
   tablespoons water

Grated Parmesan cheese

Continued on following page

SOUTHERN EGGPLANT CASSEROLE
— *Continued*

Peel eggplant and cut into slices; then soak for one hour in water to cover and ½ teaspoon salt.

Drain eggplant, dice, and put in 1-quart saucepan with cover. Add small amount of water; then cover and cook just until tender. Drain.

Heat cooking oil in small skillet; then add onion and pepper flakes and cook until soft. Combine with eggplant; then add remaining ½ teaspoon salt, pepper, bread crumbs, and egg and mix well. Pour into 2-cup baking dish and sprinkle with grated Parmesan cheese.

Bake at 350°F. for 30 minutes.

2 servings.

Sweet and Sour Green Beans

1 to 1½ cups cooked frozen, fresh, or canned green beans (reserve liquid)

2 teaspoons butter, margarine, or bacon drippings

1 tablespoon minced onion or 1 teaspoon instant chopped onion

2 strips bacon, cooked and crumbled or 1½ teaspoons imitation bacon-flavored bits

1 tablespoon cider vinegar

2 teaspoons sugar or granulated sugar replacement

¼ teaspoon salt or salt substitute

⅛ teaspoon pepper

⅛ teaspoon dried dill weed (optional)

2 tablespoons liquid from beans

Cook frozen or fresh beans or heat canned beans in 2-cup saucepan. Keep warm.

Melt butter in 1-cup saucepan. Add onion and cook until soft. Add bacon, vinegar, sugar, salt, pepper, dill, and liquid from beans; mix well and cook a few minutes. Pour over beans; reheat and serve.

2 servings.

Hominy and Cheese Casserole

The processing of hominy grits has been greatly improved, and the resultant quiet but interesting taste is worth trying.

14½-ounce can or 1½ cups hominy, drained

Salt or salt substitute

Pepper

¼ cup grated cheddar, American, or 99% fat-free cheese

2 tablespoons diced green chilies (optional)

2 tablespoons sour cream, sour cream substitute, or yogurt

2 tablespoons milk or skim, 2% fat or reconstituted dry milk

Put drained hominy in 2-cup baking dish; then sprinkle with salt and pepper. Sprinkle grated cheese, then green chilies on top.

Mix sour cream with milk in small bowl or cup. Pour over hominy.

Bake at 350°F. for 25 minutes.

2 to 3 servings.

Lentils

The honey is optional, but you will be missing something subtle, smooth, and wonderful!

¾ cup uncooked lentils

1½ cups water

½ teaspoon salt or salt substitute

⅓ cup diced carrot

⅓ cup cut-up celery

½-inch piece bay leaf

   Dash garlic powder

⅛ teaspoon dried thyme or sage

2 tablespoons honey (optional)

1 tablespoon butter or margarine

Continued on following page

LENTILS — *Continued*

Wash lentils very well and put in 1-quart saucepan with cover. Add water, salt, carrots, celery, bay leaf, garlic powder, and thyme; then mix well and cover.

Cook over medium-low heat until lentils are tender (about 45 minutes), adding more water if necessary. Add honey and butter; then mix well and keep warm in low oven.

3 servings.

ALTERNATE I: For Lentil Soup: Add 1½ cups additional water or ¾ cup water and ¾ cup canned tomatoes or tomato juice to above ingredients. One sliced frankfurter may be added, if desired.

ALTERNATE II: For Leftover Lentil Soup: Add enough bouillon, tomato soup, or water to leftover lentils for soup consistency. If desired, ¼ cup diced cooked ham, Canadian bacon, or frankfurters may be added.

Savory Lima Beans

2 teaspoons butter or margarine

1 green onion, finely chopped

2 teaspoons green pepper or 1 teaspoon
 dried sweet pepper flakes

1 tomato, peeled and seeded

 Dash of dried dill weed or thyme

¼ teaspoon salt

 Few grains pepper

1 cup frozen or canned Fordhook lima beans

Melt butter in 3-cup saucepan with cover; add onion and green pepper. Cover and cook a few minutes. Add tomatoes, dill, salt, and pepper; mix well and add lima beans. Cover and cook 10 to 15 minutes.
 2 servings.

ALTERNATE I: For Savory Green Beans: Substitute canned or frozen green beans for lima beans.

ALTERNATE II: For Savory Italian Green Beans: Substitute frozen Italian green beans for lima beans.

Imaginative Green Peas

A very quick pick-up for an ordinary meal.

- 1 cup frozen peas
- 2 tablespoons water
- 1 teaspoon butter or margarine
- 1 green onion, finely chopped
- 1 teaspoon sugar or granulated sugar replacement
- ½ teaspoon dried mint or parsley
- ¼ teaspoon salt or salt substitute

  Few grains pepper

- 2 to 3 outside lettuce leaves, finely chopped (optional, but a very exciting addition)
- 2 tablespoons sour cream or sour cream substitute

Put peas, water, butter, onion, sugar, mint, salt, and pepper in 3-cup saucepan. Cover and cook until almost tender; then add lettuce leaves and cook 5 minutes longer. Blend in sour cream, reheat and serve.

2 servings.

Easiest Potatoes

1 large potato (2-serving size) or 2 small
    potatoes

1-serving envelope instant onion soup
    or 1 cup Onion Soup (p. 30)

¾ cup hot water (if using soup mix)

   Sour cream or sour cream substitute
   (optional)

Cut off ends of potatoes and discard, but do not peel
potato. Cut potato in half; then cut into ¼-inch thick
slices. Arrange in fan shape around edges and in center of 3-cup casserole with cover.

   Mix together onion soup and hot water in small
bowl or cup. Pour over potatoes and cover.

   Bake at 350°F. for 1 to 1¼ hours. Serve with sour
cream, if desired.

   2 servings.

Potatoes in Foil

Made from ever-ready standby ingredients.

  1 tablespoon butter or margarine

  ¼ teaspoon salt or salt substitute

     Few grains pepper

  4 slices peeled potato, cut ⅛-inch thick
       (about ½ medium potato)

  3 slices onion, ⅛-inch thick

  2 tablespoons beef bouillon,
       consommé, or cream of celery soup

Using a little extra butter, grease center of 12-inch square of aluminum foil.

Mix together 1 tablespoon butter with salt and pepper.

Beginning with potato slice placed in center of foil, alternate layers of potato and onion, spreading butter mixture between each slice.

Pull foil up around stacked vegetables, add bouillon and seal completely so no steam will escape.

Bake at 350°F. for 50 to 60 minutes.

1 serving.

*Sweet Potato Casserole

1½ cups canned, frozen, or fresh-cooked, mashed sweet potatoes

1½ teaspoons maple syrup, brown sugar, or brown sugar replacement

2 teaspoons softened butter or margarine

⅛ teaspoon salt or salt substitute

Dash ground nutmeg or cinnamon

1 tablespoon orange, apple, or pineapple juice

Miniature marshmallows (optional)

Crushed cereal flakes (optional)

Combine all ingredients except marshmallows and cereal flakes in 2-cup mixing bowl. Pour into 2-cup buttered baking dish or two individual baking dishes. Top with marshmallows and/or cereal flakes.

Bake at 325°F. for about 25 minutes.

2 servings.

• Special Stuffed Sweet Potato

Will freeze well!

1 large sweet potato

¼ cup milk or skim, 2% fat or reconstituted instant dry milk

2 teaspoons butter or margarine

3 teaspoons peanut butter or diet peanut butter

2 teaspoons honey, brown sugar, or brown sugar replacement (optional)

¼ teaspoon salt or salt substitute

Few grains pepper

Wash sweet potato and cut two slits in sides to allow steam to escape.

Bake at 400°F. for one hour or until done, depending upon size of potato. Remove from oven and cut in half.

Scrape pulp from potato halves into 2-cup mixing bowl and mash until smooth; then add milk, butter, peanut butter, honey, salt, and pepper. Beat until fluffy. Refill shells and place in baking dish.

Bake about 20 minutes, or until warmed through and lightly browned on top. Run under broiler for few minutes if additional browning is desired.

2 servings.

Snow Pea Pods

1 teaspoon cornstarch

⅓ cup cold water

½ teaspoon instant chicken bouillon

1 teaspoon soy sauce

⅛ teaspoon garlic salt

2 tablespoons chopped green onions and tops

1 tablespoon butter or margarine

6-ounce package frozen snow pea pods, thawed

2-ounce can or ½ cup fresh mushrooms

Mix together cornstarch, water, chicken bouillon, soy sauce, and garlic salt in small bowl or cup. Set aside.

Cook onions in butter in 2-cup saucepan or 6-inch skillet. Add snow pea pods and mushrooms; toss and cook for a few minutes.

Add cornstarch and water mixture; then cook until sauce is thickened, being mindful to cook the peas only until just tender.

2 servings.

Flavorful Spinach

12-ounce package frozen chopped spinach

1-serving envelope onion soup mix

½ cup yogurt, sour cream, or sour cream
     substitute

Place frozen spinach in 2-cup casserole with cover; then sprinkle onion soup over top and cover.

Bake at 325°F. for about 50 minutes. Remove from oven, drain off excess liquid; then add yogurt. Mix well and return to oven until heated through.

2 servings.

Escalloped Tomatoes

A pantry shelf wonder . . . if you keep those life-savers, dried parsley, instant chopped onion, and canned tomatoes on hand . . . and you will be glad many times over if you do.

1 tablespoon butter or margarine

2 slices bread

1 teaspoon instant chopped onion or
   2 tablespoons minced onion

¼ teaspoon dried basil

¼ teaspoon dried parsley flakes

1 teaspoon sugar, brown sugar, or their
   replacements

½ teaspoon salt or salt substitute

1 cup cut-up fresh tomatoes, tomato sauce,
   or canned tomatoes

Continued on following page

ESCALLOPED TOMATOES — *Continued*

Melt butter in 2-cup stove-to-oven casserole with cover. Add bread, onion, basil, parsley, sugar, and salt; then stir well. Add tomatoes and cover.

Bake at 375°F. for 30 minutes.

2 servings.

ALTERNATE I: For Escalloped Tomatoes with Cheese: Substitute ½ cup packaged herb-seasoned dressing for bread and add ¼ cup grated cheddar, American, or 99% fat-free cheese.

ALTERNATE II: For Escalloped Tomatoes and Corn: Add ½ cup corn to either of the above recipes.

Turnip Casserole

1 pound turnips, peeled and quartered

¼ cup butter or margarine

1 tablespoon instant chopped onion or
  ¼ cup chopped onion

1 teaspoon imitation bacon bits or 1 strip
  bacon, cooked and crumbled

1 tomato, peeled and seeded

⅓ cup chopped celery (optional)

½ teaspoon salt or salt substitute

½ teaspoon sugar or granulated sugar
  replacement

¼ teaspoon fines herbes or dried sage

Few grains pepper

Cook turnips in water to cover for about 45 minutes, or until tender. Drain and mash; then add butter, onion, bacon, tomato, celery, salt, sugar, fines herbes, and pepper. Mix well. Pour into greased 2-cup baking dish.

Bake at 350°F. for about 35 minutes.

2 servings.

ALTERNATE: For Summer Squash or Zucchini Casserole: Substitute cooked and mashed summer squash or zucchini for turnips.

Special Occasion Vegetable Casserole

Become acquainted with the variety of vegetables combined in the manner of the Italians, Orientals, and French. The handy freezer bags will nicely serve two people for two meals.

18-ounce package frozen Vegetables Oriental, Vegetables Florentine, or Vegetables Italian

1 tablespoon butter or margarine

1 tablespoon flour

1 cup milk or skim, 2% fat or reconstituted instant dry milk

⅓ cup grated Parmesan cheese

½ teaspoon salt or salt substitute

Few grains pepper

¼ cup chopped almonds or water chestnuts

2 strips bacon, cooked and crumbled or 2 teaspoons imitation bacon bits (optional)

Paprika (optional)

SPECIAL OCCASION VEGETABLE CASSEROLE — *Continued*

Cook vegetables in 1-quart saucepan with cover in as little water as possible, beginning with ¼ cup, over medium-low heat.

While vegetables are cooking, blend butter with flour in 2-cup saucepan. Add milk and cook, stirring continually, until thickened. Add cheese; stir until melted and add salt and pepper.

Drain cooked vegetables and place in greased 3-cup casserole. Sprinkle vegetables with almonds and bacon. Pour cheese sauce evenly over top and sprinkle with paprika.

Bake at 350°F. for 25 minutes or until bubbling hot. **4 servings.**

RICE, PASTA, Luncheon, *and* Supper Dishes

Easy Enchiladas

15-ounce can chili con carne *without* beans

¼ cup water

4 to 6 corn tortillas, depending upon whether 2 or 3 per serving is desired

1 tablespoon cooking oil

¼ cup finely chopped onion or green onion and tops

1 cup grated longhorn, mild cheddar, American, or 99% fat-free cheese

½ cup finely shredded lettuce (optional)

Heat chili with water in 3-cup saucepan until hot; then skim fat from top, if necessary. Keep warm.

Put 2 serving plates in oven to warm.

Lightly cook tortillas, one at a time, in cooking oil, turning once.

As each tortilla is removed from cooking oil, spread with about six tablespoons chili and roll up; then place in baking dish. Continue until all tortillas are filled; then if any chili remains, pour over top. Sprinkle with cheese and onion. Bake at 350°F. for about 30 minutes. Serve with shredded lettuce, if desired.

2 to 3 servings.

Garlic Cheese Grits Casserole

⅔ cup cooked instant grits

5 ounces sharp cheddar cheese, grated

½ small clove garlic, minced

   Dash of Tabasco

2 tablespoons butter or margarine

1 teaspoon Worcestershire sauce or diet
   Worcestershire sauce (optional)

¼ teaspoon salt

   Few grains pepper

1 beaten egg, ¼ cup frozen egg substitute,
   2 tablespoons powdered egg substitute
   mixed with 2½ tablespoons water, or
   1 egg white, beaten until stiff

Cook grits in 3-cup saucepan with cover as directed
on package. Add cheese, garlic, Tabasco, butter, Worcestershire sauce, salt, and pepper; then mix well and
add egg or fold in stiffly beaten egg white. Pour into
greased 3-cup casserole.

Bake in oven preheated to 400°F. for 40 minutes.
2 servings.

Best Macaroni and Cheese

- ¾ cup uncooked elbow macaroni
- 2 tablespoons finely chopped onion
- 1½ tablespoons butter or margarine
- 1½ tablespoons flour
- ¼ teaspoon salt or salt substitute

  Few grains pepper
- ½ cup milk or skim, 2% fat or reconstituted
  instant dry milk
- ¼ cup dry white wine
- ¾ cup grated sharp cheddar or 99% fat-free
  cheese

Continued on following page

BEST MACARONI AND CHEESE
— *Continued*

Cook macaroni according to package directions; wash, drain, and set aside.

Cook onions in butter or margarine in 2-cup saucepan, stirring often, until soft. Add flour, salt, and pepper; stir until smooth. Gradually add milk, then wine, stirring constantly, until thickened. Add cheese and stir until cheese is melted and sauce is smooth.

Mix together cheese sauce and macaroni; then pour into 3-cup greased casserole.

Bake in oven preheated to 350°F. for about 30 min. **2 to 3 servings.**

ALTERNATE I: Add ½ cup diced cooked ham, Canadian bacon, or bologna.

ALTERNATE II: Add 3¼-ounce can tuna and ¼ cup chopped pimiento-filled green olives.

Notes:

Noodle Casserole

Convenient because it may be made ahead. Compatible with meat, poultry, or fish.

1½ cups boiling water

½ teaspoon salt or salt substitute

¾ cup uncooked noodles or macaroni

1 green onion and top, chopped (optional)

½ teaspoon Worcestershire sauce or diet
    Worcestershire sauce

1 tablespoon grated Parmesan cheese

½ teaspoon dried parsley flakes (optional,
    but flavorful and attractive)

Cook noodles in 3-cup saucepan in salt and water just until tender; then drain.

Add remaining ingredients and pour into greased 2-cup casserole. (May be refrigerated, if desired, and baked later.)

Bake at 350°F. for 20 to 25 minutes.

2 servings.

ALTERNATE: For Dried Beef and Noodle Casserole: Add ¼ cup cut-up sliced dried beef.

Lazy-Way Quiche

After you have made this once or twice, your imagination and ingenuity will take over and the sky will be the limit.

2 slices white or salt-free bread, toasted

1 small tomato, peeled and sliced

¾ cup grated cheddar, Swiss, American, or 99% fat-free cheese

¾ cup milk or skim, 2% fat or reconstituted instant dry milk

1 beaten egg, ¼ cup frozen egg substitute, or 2 tablespoons powdered egg substitute mix with 2½ tablespoons water

½ teaspoon salt or salt substitute

Few grains pepper

¼ teaspoon prepared mustard

Dash cayenne pepper

LAZY-WAY QUICHE — *Continued*

Cut toasted bread into cubes and arrange in bottom of greased 7-inch pie plate or casserole. Place tomato slices over bread cubes; then sprinkle tomato with grated cheese.

Mix together milk, egg, salt, pepper, mustard, and cayenne pepper in small bowl or cup. Pour over bread, tomatoes, and cheese.

Bake in preheated oven for 40 minutes.

2 servings.

ALTERNATE I: For Lazy-Way Broccoli Quiche: Substitute 3 thawed frozen or 3 cooked fresh broccoli spears for tomatoes.

ALTERNATE II: For Lazy-Way Bacon Quiche: Substitute 3 strips bacon, crisply cooked and crumbled for tomatoes and add ¼ cup finely chopped onions, if desired.

ALTERNATE III: For Lazy-Way Shrimp Quiche: Substitute ¾ cup cooked cut-up shrimp for tomatoes and Swiss or low-moisture, part-skim cheese for cheddar.

Rice Casserole

This has a beginning ... rice ... but what happens
after that is up to you as the options are practically
infinite.

⅓ cup uncooked rice

 2 tablespoons butter or margarine

¼ cup chopped onion (optional)

¼ cup chopped celery (optional)

 1 cup beef bouillon or consommé
     or 1 teaspoon beef-flavored instant
     bouillon mixed with 1 cup water

2-ounce can mushroom stems and pieces
     with liquid

 1 teaspoon salt or salt substitute

 1 teaspoon dried parsley flakes

    Dash of dried thyme or marjoram
     (optional)

¼ cup chopped green pepper or 1 teaspoon
     dried sweet pepper flakes (optional)

RICE CASSEROLE — *Continued*

Cook rice in butter in 3-cup saucepan until golden brown, stirring continually. Add onion and celery and cook until soft. Stir in remaining ingredients and pour into greased 3-cup or 1-quart casserole with cover. Size of casserole will depend on options included. Cover.

Bake at 350°F. for 45 minutes to 1 hour. May be prepared ahead, refrigerated and reheated.

2 to 3 servings.

ALTERNATE: For Beef and Rice Soup: Increase consommé or bouillon to 2½ cups.

Notes:

Rice and Cheese Casserole

1½ cups cooked rice (about ⅓ cup uncooked
     rice)

 1 small tomato, peeled, seeded, and
     chopped or ½ cup canned tomatoes or
     tomato sauce

 2 tablespoons chopped green olives stuffed
     with pimiento

¼ cup grated cheddar, pimiento, or 99%
     fat-free cheese

¼ teaspoon onion salt (optional)

    Few grains pepper

¼ teaspoon salt or salt substitute

Combine all ingredients in 3-cup bowl and mix well.
Pour into greased 3-cup casserole. Cover.
   Bake at 350°F. for 45 minutes.
   2 servings.

ALTERNATE I: For Ham, Rice and Cheese Casserole: Add ½ cup ground or finely chopped cooked
ham or Canadian bacon.

ALTERNATE II: For Mexican Rice and Cheese Casserole: Substitute diced green chilies for olives.

Meal-In-One-Soufflé Sandwich

One of the most accommodating dishes there is. Perfect for luncheon or dinner, all kinds of diets, and best made the day before it is to be served.

3 to 4 slices white, sourdough, or salt-free bread

1 cup diced cooked chicken or turkey

1 cup diced Monterey Jack or low-moisture, part-skim cheese

¼ cup mayonnaise or diet mayonnaise

¼ teaspoon salt or salt substitute

   Few grains pepper

½ cup finely chopped celery or water chestnuts

1 beaten egg, ¼ cup frozen egg substitute, or 2 tablespoons powdered egg substitute mixed with 2½ tablespoons water

¾ cup milk or skim, 2% fat or reconstituted instant dry milk

¼ cup dry white wine (optional)

Continued on following page

MEAL-IN-ONE-SOUFFLÉ SANDWICH
— *Continued*

Remove crust from bread; then cut into ½-inch cubes. Line greased 7-inch casserole with half of bread cubes.

Mix together chicken, cheese, mayonnaise, salt, pepper, and celery in 3-cup bowl. Spread over bread; then arrange remaining half bread over filling.

Mix together beaten egg, milk, and wine in same bowl; then pour over bread and filling. Refrigerate at least one-half day.

Bake in oven preheated to 350°F. for 30 to 35 min.
2 servings.

ALTERNATE I: For Crabmeat or Shrimp Meal-In-One Soufflé Sandwich: Substitute cooked shredded crabmeat or cooked, cut-up shrimp for chicken.

ALTERNATE II: For Ham and Asparagus Meal-In-One Soufflé Sandwich: Substitute cooked ham for chicken and cheddar or 99% fat-free cheese for Monterey Jack cheese and arrange 10-ounce package frozen asparagus, cooked and drained, over filling.

Spaghetti with Tomato Sauce

Since this versatile sauce keeps so well in refrigerator or freezer, you might wish to double or triple the recipe.

¼ cup finely chopped onion

1 teaspoon olive oil

1 small clove garlic, minced, or ⅛ teaspoon garlic powder

1 teaspoon dried parsley flakes (optional)

½ teaspoon salt or salt substitute

⅛ teaspoon pepper

½ teaspoon sugar or granulated sugar replacement

¼ teaspoon dried basil

8-ounce can or 1 cup tomato sauce or canned tomatoes

¼ cup fresh bread crumbs

2 tablespoons dry red or white wine (optional)

Continued on following page

SPAGHETTI WITH TOMATO SAUCE — *Continued*

2-ounce can mushroom stems and pieces
  with liquid (optional)

⅔ cup uncooked spaghetti

Cook onion in olive oil in 3-cup saucepan. Add garlic, parsley, salt, pepper, sugar, basil, tomato sauce, bread crumbs, wine, and mushrooms. Simmer over low heat for about 30 minutes. (Longer, if desired.)

Meanwhile, cook spaghetti in salted boiling water just until tender. Italian chefs add 1 teaspoon cooking oil to water to keep spaghetti from sticking together. Drain. Pour sauce over spaghetti and serve.

2 servings.

ALTERNATE I: For Spaghetti with Meat Sauce: Brown ½ pound lean ground beef, adding additional salt and pepper to taste; then drain off fat and add to tomato sauce.

ALTERNATE II: For Spaghetti with Clam Sauce: Add 6¼-ounce can clams, drained, to tomato sauce.

ALTERNATE III: For Taco Sauce: Add 2 tablespoons chopped green chilies to tomato sauce and omit basil.

Special Luncheon or Supper Sandwich

1 Holland rusk, toasted bread slice, or half
    hamburger bun
1 slice cooked ham, Canadian bacon, or
    bologna
1 slice turkey, chicken, or pressed chicken
1 slice Swiss, Monterey Jack, or
    low-moisture, part-skim cheese
1 slice tomato
2 teaspoons mayonnaise or diet mayonnaise

Place rusk, bread, or bun in baking dish lined with
aluminum foil. Alternately add sliced ham, turkey,
cheese, and tomato. Gently spread mayonnaise over
top.

   Bake at 350°F. for about 15 to 20 minutes, or until
cheese is melted and meats are warmed through.

   1 serving.

ALTERNATE I: For Mexican Luncheon or Supper
Sandwich: Substitute 1 teaspoon diced green chilies
for tomato.

ALTERNATE II: For Italian Luncheon or Supper
Sandwich: Omit mayonnaise and substitute Italian
sausage or salami for ham. Sprinkle tomato with
oregano, garlic and onion powder, top with cheese
and bake.

FRUIT

*Baked Bananas

1 banana

½ teaspoon butter or margarine

1 tablespoon brown sugar or brown sugar replacement

2 to 3 teaspoons lemon, lime, or orange juice

1 tablespoon rum, cognac, or orange liqueur (optional)

2 tablespoons shredded coconut (optional)

Ice cream, ice milk, whipped cream, or whipped low-calorie dessert topping (optional)

Peel and quarter banana; then arrange cut-side-up in bottom of small, greased baking dish.

Thinly spread butter over cut surfaces; then sprinkle alternately with brown sugar, juice, liqueur, and coconut.

Bake at 350°F. for about 20 minutes. Serve with ice cream.

2 servings.

Fresh Fruit Supreme

Why are the best things so often the simplest? Here is one that will serve you so well over and over again. The original version was made with seedless green grapes, but there's no need to think in such limited terms.

½ cup seedless green grapes; peeled, cut-up fresh peaches; peeled cut-up fresh pineapple; washed and picked-over blueberries or strawberries, or peeled, cut-up oranges

2 to 2½ tablespoons sour cream, sour cream substitute, or yogurt

2 teaspoons brown sugar or brown sugar replacement

1 teaspoon orange liqueur, rum, or brandy (optional)

FRESH FRUIT SUPREME — *Continued*

Arrange fruit in dessert dish or stemmed sherbet glass. Spread sour cream over fruit, covering to edges, if possible; then sprinkle with brown sugar and liqueur. Refrigerate about 2 hours before serving, or until brown sugar becomes caramelized in the sour cream.
  1 serving.

ALTERNATE: Fresh Fruit Supreme Salad: Substitute 1 ring fresh or canned pineapple, 2 tablespoons fresh blueberries, and 1 strawberry for fruit. Place pineapple ring on lettuce leaf and sprinkle blueberries over the pineapple. Top with sour cream sprinkled with brown sugar and use strawberry for garnish. A peeled slice of kiwi fruit is dramatic and a good substitute for blueberries or strawberry.

Notes:

Broiled Grapefruit

For meal beginnings and meal endings . . . for brunch, lunch, and dinner. For weightwatchers and for those who like to finish with a light touch.

½ grapefruit

1 tablespoon brown sugar, brown sugar
    replacement, or honey

1 teaspoon butter or margarine (optional)

1 tablespoon sherry, rum, kirsch, or brandy
    (optional)

Cut around outside edge and between sections of grapefruit; remove seeds and center.

Place grapefruit on broiler or baking pan. Sprinkle with brown sugar or honey, dot with butter and pour liquor over all.

Place about 6 inches from preheated broiler and broil about 10 minutes or bake in oven preheated to 350°F. for about 20 minutes.

1 serving.

ALTERNATE: Mix 1 tablespoon marmalade with brown sugar.

Curried Mandarin Oranges

An addition of merit to dinners with chicken, ham, or pork entreés or for brunch and luncheons.

11-ounce can mandarin oranges or diet
    mandarin oranges (reserve juice)

¼ cup juice from oranges

1 tablespoon butter or margarine

1 tablespoon brown sugar or brown sugar
   replacement

¼ teaspoon curry powder

2 teaspoons lemon juice

⅛ teaspoon salt or salt substitute

Drain mandarin oranges and set aside.

Combine juice from oranges, butter, sugar, curry powder, lemon juice, and salt in 2-cup saucepan and cook over medium-low heat for a few minutes. Add oranges and simmer about 8 minutes. Serve hot or cold. Keeps very well in refrigerator.

Makes 1½ cups.

ALTERNATE I: For Curried Mixed Salad Fruits: Substitute canned mixed salad fruits for mandarin oranges.

ALTERNATE II: For Curried Peaches: Substitute canned peaches for mandarin oranges.

Peaches or Pears in Jelly

2 fresh peaches or pears, peeled

¼ cup currant, cherry, or other tart red jelly

2 tablespoons orange juice

1 teaspoon grated orange peel

Ice cream, ice milk, whipped cream, or whipped low-calorie dessert topping (optional)

Arrange pears in 3-cup saucepan with cover; then add jelly, orange juice, and peel. Simmer over medium-low heat for 9 to 10 minutes, carefully turning pears 2 or 3 times.

Refrigerate in syrup until chilled. Serve with jelly spooned over fruit; then top with ice cream, if desired.

2 servings.

Notes:

Peaches or Pears in Wine

Leftover liquid would be good in gelatin.

  2 fresh peaches or pears

¼ cup sugar or granulated sugar replacement

¼ cup water

  2 teaspoons lemon juice

¼ teaspoon ground cinnamon

¼ cup red wine

Peel pears, leaving whole and, if possible, preserving stems.

Bring to boil sugar, water, lemon juice, cinnamon, and wine in 3-cup saucepan with cover. Place pears in liquid in a position to achieve most coverage by liquid. Cover and cook 5 minutes; then turn pears and cook 15 to 20 minutes longer. Refrigerate until thoroughly chilled.

2 servings.

Fresh Strawberries with Raspberry Sauce

Wait until you hear your guests ooh and ah over this.

1 pint fresh strawberries, washed and hulled

10-ounce package frozen red raspberries

2 tablespoons orange liqueur (optional)

Arrange strawberries in four dessert or stemmed sher-bet dishes.

Put raspberries through a sieve or blend in blender; stir in liqueur, then spoon raspberry puree over strawberries. Makes 4 servings, or if only 2 servings are desired use ½ pint berries and remaining rasp-berry puree may be used over ice cream.

Notes:

Desserts

*Apple Crisp

    4 apples, peeled and sliced

        Juice of ½ lemon

1½ tablespoons butter or margarine

 ⅓ cup brown sugar or brown sugar
        replacement

 ¼ cup unsifted flour

 ¼ teaspoon ground cinnamon

 ⅛ teaspoon ground nutmeg

 ¼ teaspoon salt or salt substitute

        Cream, polyunsaturated non-dairy cream,
        whipped cream, or low-calorie dessert
        topping

Arrange apple slices in greased 6- or 7-inch baking dish or pie plate. Sprinkle with lemon juice.

Mix butter with brown sugar, flour, cinnamon, nutmeg, and salt in small bowl or cup. Sprinkle over apples.

Bake in oven preheated to 350°F. for about 35 minutes, or until apples are tender. Top with cream.

3 to 4 servings.

ALTERNATE I: For Peach Crisp: Substitute peaches for apples.

ALTERNATE II: For Pear Crisp: Substitute pears for apples.

Berry or Fruit Dessert

A dessert that knows no season nor shows any favoritism among berries and fruits.

½ cup unsifted flour

½ cup sugar or granulated sugar replacement

½ teaspoon baking powder or low-sodium substitute

¼ teaspoon salt or salt substitute

¼ cup butter, margarine, or shortening

1 beaten egg, ¼ cup frozen egg substitute or 2 tablespoons powdered egg substitute mixed with 2½ tablespoons water

1 cup fresh, frozen or canned blueberries, blackberries, boysenberries, cherries, peaches, apples, or other fruit or berries of choice

1 teaspoon lemon juice

¼ teaspoon ground nutmeg or cinnamon, depending on choice of berries or fruit

BERRY OR FRUIT DESSERT—*Continued*

Ice cream, ice milk, low-calorie dessert
topping, frozen whipped dessert topping,
or sour cream with a little brown sugar
sprinkled on top

Mix together flour, sugar, baking powder, and salt
in 1-quart bowl. Cut butter into dry ingredients with
two knives or pastry blender; then add beaten egg.

Drain frozen or canned berries or fruit; then measure into 2-cup bowl. Mix berries or fruit with lemon
juice and nutmeg or cinnamon. Arrange fruit in bottom of greased 6- or 7-inch baking dish or pie plate;
then spread batter over berries or fruit.

Bake in oven preheated to 350°F. for 30 to 35 minutes. Serve warm or cold with topping of choice.

3 to 4 servings.

Notes:

Chocolate Delight

      1   extra large egg white or 2 egg whites

    ⅛   teaspoon cream of tartar

    ½   cup sugar or granulated sugar replacement

    ½   teaspoon vanilla extract

      4   tablespoons Chocolate Easy Pudding Mix
            (p. 258), or packaged chocolate
            pudding and pie filling, or low-calorie
            chocolate pudding and pie filling mix

  1¼   cups cold milk or skim, 2% fat or
            reconstituted instant dry milk

    ¼   cup low-calorie dessert topping mix

Beat egg whites and cream of tartar in 2-cup bowl until soft peaks form; then gradually add sugar and vanilla extract and beat until stiff. Spread in bottom and ½ inch up sides of 6- or 7-inch pie plate or baking dish.

Bake in oven preheated to 300°F. for 40 to 50 minutes, or until golden brown. Remove from oven and cool while making filling.

CHOCOLATE DELIGHT — *Continued*

Mix chocolate pudding mix with 1 cup milk in 2-cup saucepan and cook over medium-low heat, stirring continually, until thickened. Set aside.

Whip remaining ¼ cup milk with low-calorie dessert topping mix until stiff. Fold into chocolate pudding and pour into baked shell. Refrigerate.

3 to 4 servings.

ALTERNATE: For Mocha Delight: Add 2 teaspoons instant coffee or decaffeinated coffee to pudding mix.

Notes:

•Coffeemallow

¾ to 1 teaspoon instant coffee or
　　decaffeinated coffee

½ cup boiling water

2 cups miniature marshmallows

1 teaspoon cocoa or carob powder (optional)

¼ teaspoon salt or salt substitute

¼ teaspoon vanilla extract

½ cup whipped cream, sour cream, sour
　　cream substitute, or ¼ cup
　　low-calorie dessert topping whipped
　　with ¼ cup cold milk

Mix together instant coffee and boiling water in top of
double boiler. Add marshmallows, cocoa, and salt;
then stir over boiling water until marshmallows are
melted and blended into coffee. Remove from heat;
then add vanilla extract and cool.

Fold in whipped cream and pour into two sherbet
or dessert dishes or into refrigerator container with
lid. May be served with additional whipped cream
for topping, if desired.

2 servings.

ALTERNATE: For Raspberrymallow: Substitute raspberry juice for coffee and 2 teaspoons lemon juice for
vanilla extract.

Custard for Two

1 beaten egg, ¼ cup frozen egg substitute,
    2 tablespoons powdered egg substitute
    mixed with 2½ tablespoons water or
    2 egg whites

2 tablespoons sugar, granulated sugar
    replacement, brown sugar, or brown sugar
    replacement

¼ teaspoon salt or salt substitute

⅞ cup milk

⅛ teaspoon vanilla extract

    Nutmeg

    Drop yellow food coloring if using egg
      whites

Combine egg, sugar, and salt in 2-cup bowl. Add milk,
vanilla extract, and food coloring; blend vigorously.
Pour into 1½-cup baking dish; then sprinkle with
nutmeg.

    Place custard in shallow baking pan; then set pan
on oven shelf and pour boiling water into pan to
depth of ½ inch.

Continued on following page

CUSTARD FOR TWO — *Continued*

Bake in oven preheated to 350°F. for 45 minutes to 1 hour, or until knife inserted in center comes out clean.

2 servings.

ALTERNATE I: For Baked Apple Custard: Gently cook 2 apples in a little water in saucepan with cover. Drain apples and place in individual baking dishes. Pour custard over apples and bake as directed for custard.

ALTERNATE II: For Caramel Custard: Melt an additional ½ cup sugar over low heat until liquid and light golden brown. Pour into bottom of baking dish or custard cups before pouring custard into dish or dishes.

Notes:

Baked Cottage Cheese Custard

1 beaten egg, ¼ cup frozen egg substitute,
    2 tablespoons powdered egg substitute
    mixed with 2½ tablespoons water or
    2 egg whites

⅔ cup milk or skim, 2% fat or reconstituted
    instant dry milk

3 tablespoons sugar or granulated sugar
    replacement

⅛ teaspoon salt or salt substitute

¼ teaspoon vanilla, lemon, or pineapple
    extract

⅓ cup cottage cheese or low-fat cottage
    cheese

¼ cup raisins or cut-up dates

    Nutmeg

Continued on following page

BAKED COTTAGE CHEESE CUSTARD
— *Continued*

Mix egg, milk, sugar, salt, and vanilla extract in 2-cup bowl.

Mash cottage cheese and add with raisins. Pour into 1½-cup baking dish and sprinkle with nutmeg.

Place custard in shallow baking pan; then set pan on oven shelf and pour boiling water into baking pan to depth of ½ inch.

Bake in oven preheated to 350°F. for 45 minutes to 1 hour, or until knife inserted in center comes out clean.

2 servings.

ALTERNATE: For Coffee Cottage Cheese Custard: Use vanilla extract, omit nutmeg, and add ½ teaspoon instant coffee or decaffeinated coffee.

Notes:

Saltine Date Dessert

How could anything be so luscious yet remain true to most diets?

2 egg whites

⅔ cup sugar or granulated sugar replacement

½ teaspoon vanilla extract

6 finely crushed saltine crackers or salt-free saltine crackers

6 finely chopped dates

¼ cup finely chopped nuts or toasted soy nuts

Whipped low-calorie dessert topping or whipped cream

Beat egg whites until stiff in 3-cup mixing bowl. Gradually add sugar; then vanilla extract. Fold in crackers, dates, and nuts.

Pour into greased 6- or 7-inch baking dish or pie plate.

Bake in oven preheated to 325°F. for 20 to 25 minutes. Serve warm with whipped dessert topping.

2 servings.

Fruit Gelatin Cream

There is hardly an easier answer to a good dessert, especially one that keeps well. The newest diet fruit gelatins meet the requirements of those on a low-sodium as well as sugar-restricted diet.

¾ cup water

3-ounce package fruit-flavored gelatin or
    4-serving envelope low-calorie,
    low-sodium fruit-flavored gelatin
    dessert

8-ounce can crushed unsweetened
    pineapple and juice

1½ cups vanilla-flavored ice cream, ice milk,
    or dietetic pack ice cream

Heat water to boiling in 3-cup saucepan; then add gelatin. Remove from heat; stir until gelatin is dissolved and add pineapple with juice. Stir in ice cream. Pour into 1-quart refrigerator container with lid, four 6-ounce containers with lids, or four dessert dishes. Refrigerate until firm.

   4 servings.

Caramel Dumplings

SAUCE:

¾ cup sugar or granulated sugar replacement

1 cup boiling water

1 tablespoon butter or margarine

¼ teaspoon salt or salt substitute

Caramelize ¼ cup sugar by melting over low heat in heavy small pan or skillet until liquid and golden brown. Add boiling water, ½ cup sugar, butter, and salt; then cook over medium-low heat for about 10 minutes. Pour into greased 7-inch baking dish or pie plate.

Continued on following page

CARAMEL DUMPLINGS — *Continued*

DUMPLINGS:

1 tablespoon butter or margarine

¼ cup sugar or granulated sugar replacement

¾ cup unsifted flour

1 teaspoon baking powder or low-sodium substitute

¼ cup milk or skim, 2% fat or reconstituted instant dry milk

½ teaspoon vanilla extract

Whipped cream, low-calorie dessert topping or frozen dessert topping

Cream butter with sugar in 2-cup bowl.

Mix flour with baking powder and add to creamed mixture alternately with milk. Add vanilla extract. Drop by spoonfuls into caramel sauce.

Bake in oven preheated to 350°F. for about 30 minutes. Serve warm with whipped cream or topping.

3 to 4 servings.

Spanish Cream

1½ teaspoons unflavored gelatin

 1 cup milk or skim, 2% fat or reconstituted
   instant dry milk

 3 tablespoons sugar or granulated sugar
   replacement

⅛ teaspoon salt or salt substitute

 1 egg, separated

½ teaspoon vanilla extract

   Fresh sliced fruit, berries, or cooked
   fruit or berry sauce

Sprinkle gelatin over milk in 2-cup saucepan and let stand 5 minutes. Add sugar and salt; then cook over medium-low heat until gelatin and sugar are dissolved.

Beat egg yolk slightly; then add a little hot milk to egg yolk. Add egg yolk very slowly to milk and cook, stirring continually, until mixture coats spoon and is thickened. Cool.

Beat egg white until stiff; then add vanilla extract. Fold egg white into custard and pour into 2-cup mold or bowl. Refrigerate until firm. Serve with fresh fruit or berries or cooked fruit or berry sauce.

2 servings.

Continued on following page

SPANISH CREAM — *Continued*

ALTERNATE I: For Chocolate Spanish Cream: Add ½-ounce unsweetened chocolate to hot milk. Serve with whipped cream or low-calorie dessert topping.

ALTERNATE II: For Orange Spanish Cream: Substitute ½ cup orange juice for ½ cup milk and add 1 teaspoon grated orange rind.

Notes:

Fudge Pie

One man said, "The only kind of dessert is chocolate," and another man ate one-half of this pie at one sitting, so it isn't always a 4-serving dessert.

¼ cup margarine or butter

1 ounce unsweetened chocolate

⅓ cup sugar or granulated sugar replacement

2 tablespoons unsifted flour

1 egg, ¼ cup frozen egg substitute, or 2 tablespoons powdered egg substitute mixed with 2½ tablespoons water

¼ teaspoon vanilla extract

Few drops imitation butter flavoring, if margarine is used (optional)

Ice cream, ice milk, whipped cream, or whipped low-calorie dessert topping

Melt margarine with chocolate in 3-cup saucepan. Remove from heat.

Measure sugar into measuring cup; then add flour and mix well. Blend sugar mixture thoroughly with chocolate; then beat in egg, vanilla extract, and butter flavoring. Pour into greased 6- or 7-inch pie plate.

Bake in oven preheated to 300°F. for 25 to 30 minutes, or until center springs back when pressed with finger. Serve with ice cream, ice milk, whipped cream, or whipped low-calorie dessert topping.

4 servings.

Dandy Pudding

No one will ever know this was made with crumbs from not-too-fresh sweet-rolls, doughnuts, cookies, coffeecake, or cake.

- 1 cup milk or skim, 2% fat or reconstituted instant dry milk
- 1 cup less-than-fresh sweet-roll, doughnut, coffeecake, cookie, or cake crumbs
- 2 egg whites, 1 egg, ¼ cup frozen egg substitute or 2 tablespoons powdered egg substitute mixed with 2½ tablespoons water
- 2 tablespoons sugar, granulated sugar replacement, brown sugar, brown sugar replacement, or honey
- ⅛ teaspoon ground cinnamon
- ⅛ teaspoon ground nutmeg
- ¼ cup chopped nuts (optional)
- ¼ cup chopped dates, apples, or raisins (optional)

DANDY PUDDING — *Continued*

Pour milk over crumbs in 1-quart bowl and let stand a few minutes.

Beat egg whites or egg with sugar and add to crumb mixture; stir in cinnamon and nutmeg; then add nuts and dates. Pour into greased 3-cup baking dish.

Bake in oven preheated to 375°F. for 40 minutes, or until knife inserted in center comes out clean. Serve with sauce made from leftover fruit juice and thickened with a little cornstarch, maple syrup, cream, ice cream, whipped cream, or low-calorie dessert topping.

2 to 3 servings.

ALTERNATE I: For Chocolate Dandy Pudding: Heat milk with ½ ounce unsweetened chocolate or 1 tablespoon cocoa or carob powder and 1 teaspoon butter or margarine; then soak crumbs in milk-chocolate mixture.

ALTERNATE II: For Lemon Dandy Pudding: Add ¼ teaspoon lemon extract or 1 tablespoon fresh lemon juice and a little grated lemon rind.

Easy Pudding Mix

2 tablespoons cornstarch

4 tablespoons sugar or granulated sugar
   replacement

⅛ teaspoon salt or salt substitute (optional)

Mix together all ingredients; then pour into jar or plastic container with lid and store until needed.

To make 1 serving of pudding: Dissolve 2 tablespoons Easy Pudding Mix in ½ cup milk and cook over medium-low heat, stirring frequently, until thickened (about 20 minutes). Remove from heat and add ⅛ teaspoon vanilla extract.

ALTERNATE: For Chocolate Easy Pudding Mix: Add 1 tablespoon cocoa or carob powder to cornstarch and sugar. To make pudding, increase Easy Pudding Mix to 2 tablespoons, plus 1 teaspoon.

How to Make Pudding for One from Packaged Mixes

If you are on a salt-free diet, the commercial mixes contain salt and are not for you, but you may make your own pudding mix by following directions for Easy Pudding Mix.

2 tablespoons plus 1 teaspoon packaged instant pudding and pie filling mixed with ½ cup milk or skim, 2% fat or reconstituted instant dry milk, equals 1 serving.

2 tablespoons plus 1 teaspoon packaged pudding and pie filling mixed with ½ cup milk or skim, 2% fat or reconstituted instant dry milk; then cooked over medium-low heat until thickened, equals 1 serving.

1 scant tablespoon packaged low-calorie pudding and pie filling mixed with ½ cup milk or skim, 2% fat or reconstituted instant dry milk; then cooked over medium-low heat until thickened, equals 1 serving.

Tapioca Pudding

1½ cups milk or skim, 2% fat or reconstituted
      instant dry milk

 1 tablespoon minute tapioca

⅓ cup sugar or granulated sugar replacement

⅛ teaspoon salt or salt substitute

 1 beaten egg, ¼ cup frozen egg substitute,
      or 2 tablespoons powdered egg
      substitute mixed with 2½ tablespoons
      water

½ teaspoon vanilla extract

Heat milk in 3-cup saucepan; then add tapioca and
cook until tapioca is transparent.

Add sugar and salt to beaten egg and pour into hot
milk, stirring continually. Cook over medium-low
heat, stirring continually, until thickened. Pour into
bowl or sherbet glasses and refrigerate.

About 3 servings.

TAPIOCA PUDDING — *Continued*

ALTERNATE I: For Chocolate Tapioca Pudding: Add 1 tablespoon cocoa or carob powder mixed with 1 teaspoon butter or margarine to hot milk and tapioca mixture; or add ⅓ cup semisweet chocolate bits after eggs have been added to milk mixture.

ALTERNATE II: For Banana Tapioca Pudding: Add ½ cup chopped bananas to cooked pudding.

ALTERNATE III: For Pineapple Tapioca Pudding: Substitute ½ cup juice from pineapple for ½ cup milk and add ½ cup very well-drained crushed pineapple.

Notes:

Fresh Berry Soufflé

If you haven't an electric blender, it is easy to pureé berries by cutting through them in a whipping motion with a small paring knife.

1½ teaspoons unflavored gelatin

½ to ¾ cup sugar or granulated sugar replacement (depending on sweetness of berries)

¼ cup water

1 teaspoon lemon juice

¼ teaspoon vanilla extract

1 cup cut-up strawberries or raspberries, mashed or pureéd

1 egg white

¼ cup low-calorie dessert topping mix whipped with ¼ cup cold milk or ½ cup whipping cream, whipped

FRESH BERRY SOUFFLE — *Continued*

Mix gelatin and sugar together in 3-cup saucepan. Add water and dissolve gelatin over medium-low heat; then cool.

·Add lemon juice, vanilla extract, and mashed or pureéd berries; refrigerate while beating egg white.

Beat egg white until soft peaks form and fold into berry mixture; then fold in whipped dessert topping. Refrigerate until firm.

2 to 3 servings.

ALTERNATE: For Fresh Berry Chiffon Pie or Tarts: Make 1 recipe Fresh Berry Soufflé and fill one 6- or 7-inch baked pie shell or four tart shells.

Notes:

Lemon Sponge

Feathery light and refreshing. In tune with all diets.

 2 egg whites

½ cup sugar or granulated sugar replacement

¼ teaspoon salt or salt substitute

1½ tablespoons flour

 1 tablespoon softened butter or margarine

¼ cup lemon juice (about 1 lemon)

 1 teaspoon grated lemon rind

½ cup milk or skim, 2% fat or reconstituted instant dry milk

Beat egg whites in 2-cup bowl until soft peaks form; then add 2 tablespoons sugar and beat until stiff.

Combine salt and flour with remaining sugar in 1-quart bowl; then rub in butter with spoon. Add lemon juice and rind; mix well and add milk. Fold in egg whites. Pour into 3-cup baking dish.

Place baking dish with lemon sponge in shallow baking pan; then set pan on oven shelf and pour boiling water into pan to depth of ½ inch.

Bake in oven preheated to 350°F. for about 45 min.
3 to 4 servings.

English Trifle

Things of value perpetuate themselves as has this fine old dessert devised from practicality, but suitable for the most elegant occasion.

4 whole ladyfingers or equivalent in fingers
    of pound, angelfood, or sponge cake
  Currant, cherry, strawberry, raspberry, or
    apricot jelly
2 tablespoons plus 1 teaspoon sherry or
    orange liqueur
2 tablespoons Easy Pudding Mix (p. 258),
    or packaged vanilla pudding and pie
    filling or low-calorie vanilla pudding and
    pie filling mix
¾ cup milk or skim, 2% fat or reconstituted
    instant dry milk

Open ladyfingers and spread inside surfaces with jelly; then put back together and cut in half. Arrange 4 ladyfinger halves in each of two sherbet glasses or dessert dishes. Sprinkle ladyfingers in each glass with sherry or liqueur, using 1 tablespoon for each.

Mix together pudding mix and milk in 2-cup saucepan. Cook over medium-low heat, stirring continually, until thickened. Pour half of the pudding into each glass over the ladyfingers. Refrigerate until well chilled.

2 servings.

Rosé Wine Gelatin Dessert

Recipe may be easily reduced by cutting ingredient measurements in half.

1 envelope unflavored gelatin

2 tablespoons sugar or granulated sugar replacement

2 cups rosé wine

1 cup fresh, sliced strawberries or peaches, or canned, drained Royal Ann cherries, fruit cocktail, or other fruit of choice

Whipped cream or whipped low-calorie dessert topping

Mix gelatin and sugar together in 3-cup saucepan, then add ½ cup wine. Stir over low heat until gelatin is dissolved. Remove from heat and add remaining wine. Refrigerate until consistency of unbeaten egg white.

Fold fruit into gelatin and spoon into wine or sherbet glasses. Refrigerate. Serve with whipped cream or low-calorie dessert topping.

Makes 3 servings in sherbet glasses or 4 servings in wine glasses.

Quick Breads

Applesauce Bread

If you are on a low-sodium diet, supermarkets, health food and drug stores have reliable substitutes for baking powder and baking soda.

⅔ cup unsifted flour

¼ cup firmly packed brown sugar or brown sugar replacement

½ teaspoon baking soda or low-sodium substitute

½ teaspoon baking powder or low-sodium substitute

½ teaspoon salt or salt substitute

½ teaspoon ground cinnamon

¼ teaspoon ground nutmeg

½ cup quick-cooking rolled oats

1 egg, ¼ cup frozen egg substitute, or 2 tablespoons powdered egg substitute mixed in 2½ tablespoons water

3 tablespoons cooking oil

½ cup applesauce

½ cup chopped nuts, dates, or raisins

Continued on following page

APPLESAUSE BREAD — *Continued*

Mix together flour, brown sugar, soda, baking powder, salt, cinnamon, nutmeg, and oats in 1-quart mixing bowl.

Beat egg in measuring cup or small bowl; then add cooking oil and applesauce.

Pour egg mixture into dry ingredients, stirring only until dry ingredients are moistened. Fold in nuts, dates, or raisins.

Pour batter into greased 1-pound coffee can or 7½ x 3½ x 2¼-inch loaf pan. Bake in oven preheated to 350°F. for about 50 minutes, coffee can; about 30 minutes for loaf pan, or until toothpick inserted in center comes out clean.

Makes 8 to 10 thin slices.

Notes:

Biscuits

¾ cup unsifted flour

1½ tablespoons instant dry milk

1½ teaspoons baking powder or low-sodium substitute

¼ teaspoon salt or salt substitute

2 tablespoons margarine or shortening

¼ to ⅓ cup water

Mix together flour, instant dry milk, baking powder, and salt in 2-cup mixing bowl.

Cut margarine into dry ingredients with 2 table knives or pasty blender; then sprinkle water over dry ingredients and mix just until dough is moistened.

Sprinkle 12-inch square of aluminum foil or plastic wrap with flour. Press out or roll out dough into ½-inch thickness. Cut desired size biscuits and place on ungreased baking pan.

Bake in oven preheated to 425°F. for about 15 min. **Makes five 2-inch biscuits.**

ALTERNATE I: For Shortcake: Add 2 tablespoons sugar or granulated sugar replacement.

ALTERNATE II: For Herb Biscuits: Add ¼ teaspoon mixed herbs and ½ teaspoon dried parsley flakes.

ALTERNATE III: For Cheese Biscuits: Add ¼ cup grated cheddar, American, or 99% fat-free cheese.

ALTERNATE IV: For Ham or Bacon Biscuits: Add ¼ cup finely chopped cooked ham or crisply cooked and crumbled bacon.

Quick Biscuit Loaf

Not only is this delicious way of glamorizing biscuits unusual, but also it is practical as it eliminates the need for bread and butter plates and butter.

5- or 6-package refrigerated biscuits

5 or 6 pieces, 1½-inch square, cheddar, Monterey Jack, American, low-moisture, low-fat or 99% fat-free cheese

1 green onion and top, finely chopped

Stand first biscuit on its edge in greased 6⅛ x 3¾ x 2-inch foil loaf pan or baking dish equivalent. Stand first piece of cheese on its edge next to biscuit; then repeat until all biscuits and squares of cheese have been alternately put in place.

Sprinkle onion between each biscuit by separating the sections slightly with a knife.

Bake in oven preheated to 400°F. for 12 to 15 min.

ALTERNATE: For Quick Herb Biscuit Loaf: Omit cheese and mix 2 tablespoons softened butter or margarine with 1 teaspoon dried parsley flakes or ¼ teaspoon mixed herbs. Spread biscuits with butter mixture and arrange in pan.

Whole Wheat Banana Bread

⅓ cup shortening

⅔ cup firmly packed brown sugar or brown
    sugar replacement

1 beaten egg, ¼ cup frozen egg substitute,
    or 2 tablespoons powdered egg
    substitute mixed with 2½ tablespoons
    water

1 large banana, mashed

1 cup whole wheat flour

¼ teaspoon salt or salt substitute

½ teaspoon baking soda or low-sodium
    substitute

1 teaspoon baking powder or low-sodium
    substitute

⅓ cup water

⅓ cup chopped nuts or toasted soy nuts

Continued on following page

WHOLE WHEAT BANANA BREAD — *Continued*

Cream shortening, sugar, and eggs in 1-quart bowl. Add banana and mix well.

Mix together flour, salt, soda, and baking powder in small bowl.

Add dry ingredients alternately with water to creamed mixture. Pour into greased 7½ x 3½ x 2¼-inch loaf pan.

Bake in oven preheated to 350°F. for about 30 minutes, or until center springs back when pressed with finger.

Makes 8 to 10 thin slices.

Notes:

Lemon Bread

1¾ cups unsifted flour

¼ teaspoon baking soda or low-sodium substitute

1½ teaspoons baking powder or low-sodium substitute

¼ teaspoon salt or salt substitute

3 tablespoons shortening

½ cup sugar or granulated sugar replacement

¼ cup wheat germ

2 tablespoons grated lemon rind

1 beaten egg, ¼ cup frozen egg substitute, or 2 tablespoons powdered egg substitute mixed with 2½ tablespoons water

¼ cup lemon juice

¼ cup milk or skim, 2% fat or reconstituted instant dry milk

Continued on following page

LEMON BREAD — *Continued*

Mix flour, soda, baking powder, and salt into 1-quart bowl; then mix shortening with dry ingredients with fingers or spoon. Add sugar and wheat germ; mix well.

Combine lemon rind, beaten egg, lemon juice, and milk in small bowl. Pour into dry ingredients and mix just until moistened. Pour into greased 7½x3½x2¼-inch loaf pan.

Bake in oven preheated to 350°F. for about 30 minutes, or until center springs back when pressed with finger.

Makes 8 to 10 thin slices.

ALTERNATE: For Orange Bread: Substitute orange rind and orange juice for lemon rind and lemon juice.

Notes:

Pumpkin Bread

¾ cup sugar or granulated sugar replacement

¼ cup cooking oil

1 beaten egg, ¼ cup frozen egg substitute,
   or 2 tablespoons powdered egg substitute
   mixed with 2½ tablespoons water

¼ cup water

⅓ cup cooked pumpkin

½ teaspoon baking soda or low-sodium
   substitute

1 cup unsifted flour

½ teaspoon salt or salt substitute

¼ teaspoon ground cinnamon

¼ teaspoon ground nutmeg

¼ teaspoon ground ginger (optional)

½ cup nuts, high-protein cereal flakes, or
   toasted soy nuts

Continued on following page

PUMPKIN BREAD — *Continued*

Measure sugar into 1-quart mixing bowl.

Mix together cooking oil, egg, water, pumpkin, and soda in 2-cup bowl; then blend into sugar.

Combine flour, salt, cinnamon, nutmeg, and ginger in measuring cup; then quickly add to liquid mixture and blend well. Add nuts and pour into greased 7½ x 3½ x 2¼-inch loaf pan.

Bake in oven preheated to 350°F. for about 30 minutes, or until center springs back when pressed with finger.

Makes 8 to 10 thin slices.

Notes:

Basic Coffeecake

One-half cup blueberries, cherries, apples, or peaches would be good added to this basic batter — as would nutmeats sprinkled over the top.

 1 cup unsifted flour

 2 teaspoons baking powder or low-sodium
       substitute

¼ teaspoon salt or salt substitute

 2 tablespoons sugar or granulated sugar
       replacement

 2 tablespoons butter or margarine

¼ teaspoon imitation butter flavoring,
       if using margarine (optional)

 2 egg whites or 1 egg, ¼ cup frozen egg
       substitute or 2 tablespoons powdered
       egg substitute mixed with
       2½ tablespoons water

    Milk

¼ teaspoon vanilla extract

Continued on following page

BASIC COFFEECAKE — *Continued*

Mix together flour, baking powder, salt, and sugar in 1-quart bowl; then blend in butter.

Mix together egg whites or egg with milk to make 1 cup; add vanilla extract. Pour over dry ingredients, mixing until blended. Pour batter into greased 7-inch square pan or equivalent.

Bake in oven preheated to 250°F. for 25 minutes. **Makes four 3-inch x 3-inch servings.**

TOPPING

- 2 tablespoons sugar or granulated sugar replacement
- 1 tablespoon butter or margarine
- 1 tablespoon flour
- 1 teaspoon ground cinnamon

Mix together sugar, butter, flour, and cinnamon in small bowl or cup. Sprinkle over coffeecake batter.

Spice Coffeecake

    1 cup unsifted flour
    ½ cup firmly packed brown sugar or brown
          sugar replacement
    ⅓ cup butter or margarine
    ¼ teaspoon imitation butter flavoring,
          if using margarine (optional)
    1 egg, ¼ cup frozen egg substitute, or 2
          tablespoons powdered egg substitute
          mixed with 2½ tablespoons water
    ⅓ cup buttermilk
    ½ teaspoon baking soda or low-sodium
          substitute
    ½ teaspoon ground cinnamon
    ¼ teaspoon ground cloves
    ¼ teaspoon salt or salt substitute
    ½ cup nuts or toasted soy nuts
    ½ cup cut-up dates or raisins (optional)

Mix together with fingers or spoon flour, sugar, and
butter in 1-quart bowl. Set aside ½ cup for topping.

Add egg, buttermilk, soda, cinnamon, cloves, and
salt; blend very well. Fold in nuts and dates. Pour into
greased 7-inch square pan or equivalent.

Bake in oven preheated to 350°F. for 30 to 35 min.
Makes four 3-inch x 3-inch pieces.

Cornbread

If you have leftover cornbread, make stuffing for poultry or serve creamed chicken over reheated cornbread.

¾ cup cornmeal

¼ cup unsifted flour

¼ teaspoon baking soda or low-sodium substitute

¼ teaspoon salt or salt substitute

1 teaspoon sugar or granulated sugar replacement

1 tablespoon melted margarine or shortening

1 beaten egg, ¼ cup frozen egg substitute, or 2 tablespoons powdered egg substitute mixed with 2½ tablespoons water

⅓ cup buttermilk

Mix together cornmeal, flour, soda, salt, and sugar in 2-cup bowl.

Combine melted margarine, beaten egg, and buttermilk; then pour into dry ingredients and mix just until moistened. Spread in greased 6- or 7-inch square pan or pie plate.

Bake in oven preheated to 425°F. for 20 to 25 min. **Makes four 3-inch x 3-inch pieces.**

ALTERNATE: For Jalapeño Cornbread: Add 1 tablespoon diced green chilies to batter.

● **Muffins**

What is your pleasure? A delicately flavored, light-as-air muffin? Then this is it. If you add ½ cup chopped dates, nuts, raisins, blueberries, apples, or cranberries you have the same good beginning with all kinds of interesting endings.

   1   cup unsifted flour

1½   teaspoons baking powder or low-sodium substitute

   2   tablespoons sugar or granulated sugar replacement

 ¼   teaspoon salt or salt substitute

   1   egg white or 2 tablespoons frozen egg substitute

   2   tablespoons softened margarine or cooking oil

 ½   cup milk or skim, 2% fat or reconstituted instant dry milk

 ¼   teaspoon imitation butter flavoring (optional)

Continued on following page

MUFFINS — *Continued*

Mix together flour, baking powder, sugar, and salt in 1-quart bowl.

Beat egg white in measuring cup; then add margarine, milk, and butter flavoring. Pour into dry ingredients and mix just until moistened.

Grease muffin tins or line with paper baking cups; then fill two-thirds full with batter.

Bake in oven preheated to 400°F. for 20 minutes, or until golden brown.

Makes six 2½-inch muffins.

ALTERNATE: For Orange Marmalade Muffins: Substitute orange juice for milk and put 1 teaspoon orange marmalade on top of each muffin before baking.

Notes:

⁕Popovers

What fun! One measuring cup, a few beats with a spoon and pop ! ! ! overs.

⅓ cup unsifted flour

¼ teaspoon salt or salt substitute

⅓ cup milk or skim, 2% fat or reconstituted
    instant dry milk

1 egg or 2 egg whites

Put all ingredients in measuring cup or small bowl and beat just until smooth.

Pour batter into well-greased muffin tins or custard cups, filling one-half full.

Bake in oven preheated to 450°F. for 20 minutes; then reduce heat to 350°F. and bake 25 min. longer.

Makes 4 popovers.

Yeast Breads

Cinnamon-Raisin Bread

Cinnamon rolls or coffee cake may be made from this sweet dough.

2¾ to 3 cups unsifted flour

¼ cup sugar or granulated sugar replacement

1 teaspoon salt or salt substitute

1 teaspoon ground cinnamon

1 package active dry yeast

1 cup milk or skim, 2% fat or reconstituted instant dry milk

2 tablespoons margarine or butter

1 teaspoon grated lemon rind (optional)

½ cup raisins

Mix together 1½ cups flour, sugar, salt, cinnamon, and yeast in 2-quart bowl.

Heat milk, margarine, and lemon rind in 2-cup saucepan until about 125°F., or until temperature of warm bath water. Pour into dry ingredients and beat with electric mixer at medium speed for 2 minutes, or with wooden spoon until consistency of smooth cake batter. Gradually add ½ cup more flour and mix with mixer or spoon again. Remove all dough from

Continued on following page

CINNAMON-RAISIN BREAD—*Continued*

beaters or spoon; then add raisins with remaining flour and knead with fingers until all flour has been absorbed into dough, or about 8 to 10 minutes. The bowl sides will be clean and the dough will not be sticky, but firm and manageable.

Form dough into ball and grease on all sides. Put dough into bowl and cover with damp cloth. Let rise in warm place (85°F.) until doubled in bulk, or 1 to 1¼ hours.

Punch down dough and knead very vigorously for several minutes; then shape into ball and put into bowl. Cover with damp cloth. Let rise for 15 minutes; then knead vigorously and form into oval-shape ball. Place in 8½ x 4½ x 2½-inch greased loaf pan; or form two equal-size, oval-shape balls and place in two greased, 6 x 3¾ x 2-inch foil loaf pans. Grease exposed surface, cover with damp cloth and let rise until doubled in bulk, or 1 to 1¼ hours.

Bake in oven preheated to 400°F. for about 30 minutes, or until done, depending on pan size. Remove from pans immediately and cool. Keeps very well under refrigeration, or in freezer.

Makes one 8½x4½x2½-inch loaf or two 6x3¾x2-inch loaves.

ALTERNATE: For Onion-Dill Bread: Substitute 1 teaspoon dried dill weed for cinnamon and 1 tablespoon instant chopped onion for raisins. May be baked in greased, 1-quart casserole, if desired.

Quick-Mix Rye Bread

Love's labor is never lost when it comes to making bread. However, the new speedy-mix way is a welcome advantage.

2½ to 3 cups unsifted rye flour

1½ teaspoons salt or salt substitute

1 package active dry yeast

1 cup milk or skim, 2% fat or reconstituted instant dry milk

2 tablespoons honey or molasses

2 tablespoons butter or margarine

2 teaspoons cocoa or carob powder (optional)

1 tablespoon caraway seed (optional)

1 tablespoon cornmeal (optional)

Mix together 1½ cups flour, salt, and yeast in 2-quart bowl.

Heat milk, honey, and margarine in 2-cup saucepan until about 125°F., or temperature of warm bath water. Pour into dry ingredients and beat with electric mixer at medium speed for 2 minutes, or with wooden

Continued on following page

QUICK-MIX RYE BREAD — *Continued*

spoon until consistency of smooth cake batter. Gradually add ½ cup more flour and mix with mixer or spoon again. Remove all dough from beaters or spoon; then add remaining flour, cocoa, and caraway seeds and knead with fingers until all flour has been absorbed into dough, or about 8 to 10 minutes. The bowl sides will be clean, and the dough will not be sticky, but firm and manageable.

Form dough into ball and grease on all sides. Put dough into bowl and cover with damp cloth. Let rise in warm place (85°F.) until doubled in bulk or 1½ to 2 hours.

Punch down dough and knead very vigorously for several minutes; then shape into ball and put into bowl. Cover with damp cloth. Let rise for 15 minutes; then knead vigorously and form into 6-inch long oval.

Grease cookie sheet or baking dish and sprinkle with cornmeal. Place dough on cornmeal. Grease top and sides of bread; then cover with cloth. Let rise until doubled in bulk, or about 1¼ hours.

Bake in oven preheated to 400°F. for 35 to 40 minutes. Remove from pan and let cool.

Makes one 8 x 3-inch loaf.

White Bread

3 cups unsifted flour

1½ tablespoons sugar or granulated sugar replacement

1¼ teaspoons salt or salt substitute

1 package active dry yeast

1 cup milk or skim, 2% fat or reconstituted instant dry milk

3 tablespoons butter or margarine

Mix together 1½ cups flour, sugar, salt, and yeast in 2-quart bowl.

Heat milk and butter in 2-cup saucepan until about 125°F., or until temperature of warm bath water. Pour into dry ingredients and beat with electric mixer at medium speed for 2 minutes, or with wooden spoon until consistency of smooth cake batter. Gradually add ½ cup more flour and mix with mixer or spoon again. Remove all dough from beaters or spoon; then add remaining flour and knead with fingers until all flour has been absorbed into dough, or about 8 to 10 minutes. The bowl sides will be clean, and the dough will not be sticky, but firm and manageable.

Continued on following page

WHITE BREAD — *Continued*

Form dough into ball and grease on all sides. Put dough into bowl and cover with damp cloth. Let rise in warm place (85°F.) until doubled in bulk, or 1 to 1¼ hours.

Punch down dough and knead very vigorously for several minutes; then shape into ball and put into bowl. Cover with damp cloth. Let rise for 15 minutes; then knead vigorously and form into oval-shape ball. Place in greased 8½ x 4½ x 2½-inch loaf pan; or form two equal-size, oval-shape balls and place in two greased, 6 x 3¾ x 2-inch foil loaf pans. Grease exposed surface, cover with damp cloth and let rise until doubled in bulk, or 1 to 1¼ hours.

Bake in oven preheated to 400°F. for about 30 minutes, or until done, depending upon pan size. Remove from pans immediately and cool. Freezes well.

Makes one 8½x4½x2½-inch loaf or two 6x3¾x2-inch loaves.

ALTERNATE: For Christmas Bread: Increase sugar to ½ cup and add ½ teaspoon ground nutmeg or cardamom, ½ cup raisins and ¼ cup diced citron.

Cakes

Kentucky Butter Cake

This heavenly cake has its own sauce or may be the perfect base for crushed fruit, chocolate, or butterscotch sauce.

½ cup margarine or butter

1 cup sugar or granulated sugar replacement

2 beaten eggs, ½ cup frozen egg substitute or 2-egg size envelope powdered egg substitute mixed with ⅓ cup water

1⅓ cups unsifted flour

½ teaspoon baking powder or low-sodium substitute

¼ teaspoon baking soda or low-sodium substitute

½ teaspoon salt or salt substitute

¼ teaspoon imitation butter flavoring, if margarine is used

1 teaspoon vanilla extract

½ cup buttermilk or milk, skim, 2% fat or reconstituted instant dry milk mixed with 2 teaspoons vinegar

¼ cup grated chocolate (optional)

Continued on following page

KENTUCKY BUTTER CAKE — *Continued*

Cream margarine with sugar in 1-quart bowl. Add eggs and mix well.

Mix together flour, baking powder, soda, and salt; then add to creamed mixture alternately with butter flavoring and vanilla extract mixed with buttermilk. Fold in grated chocolate. Stir until smooth and pour into greased 1½-quart baking dish.

Bake in oven preheated to 325°F. for about 45 minutes or until center springs back when pressed with finger. Serve with sauce, crushed fruit, chocolate, or butterscotch sauce.

Makes six 2½ x 3-inch pieces.

Notes:

°Sauce for Kentucky Butter Cake

½ cup sugar or granulated sugar replacement

¼ cup butter or margarine

2 tablespoons water

½ teaspoon vanilla extract

¼ teaspoon imitation butter flavoring,
    if margarine is used

Combine all ingredients in 1-cup saucepan; then bring just to boiling. Add vanilla and butter flavoring and pour over hot cake.

Notes:

Carrot Cake

1   cup sugar or granulated sugar replacement

⅔   cup cooking oil

2   eggs, ½ cup frozen egg substitute, or
    2-egg size envelope powdered egg
    substitute mixed with ⅓ cup water

1   cup unsifted flour

1   teaspoon baking soda or low-sodium
    substitute

1   teaspoon ground cinnamon

½   teaspoon salt or salt substitute

1½   cups grated carrots (about 1½ carrots)

½   cup chopped nuts or toasted soy nuts

Mix together sugar, oil, and eggs in 1-quart bowl, stirring until well-blended and sugar is dissolved.

Mix together flour, soda, cinnamon, and salt; then gradually add to sugar mixture, stirring until thoroughly blended. Fold in carrots and nuts. Pour into greased 1½-quart baking dish.

Bake in oven preheated to 350°F. for about 30 minutes. Cool and frost with Cream Cheese Frosting.

Makes six 2½ x 3-inch pieces.

Continued on following page

CARROT CAKE — *Continued*

CREAM CHEESE FROSTING

3-ounce package cream cheese or
    lowered-calorie cream cheese

¼ cup margarine or butter

½ teaspoon vanilla extract

2 to 2½ cups powdered sugar

Mix together cream cheese, margarine, and vanilla extract in 1-quart mixing bowl. Gradually add powdered sugar, blending until smooth.

Frosts one 5 x 9-inch cake.

Notes:

Quick Chocolate Cake

If chocolate is off-limits for you, carob powder is a satisfying stand-in.

1   cup unsifted flour

1   cup sugar or granulated sugar replacement

1   teaspoon baking soda or low-sodium
      substitute

¼   teaspoon salt or salt substitute

5   tablespoons cocoa or carob powder

¼   teaspoon ground cinnamon

½   cup cooking oil

½   cup buttermilk or milk, skim, 2% fat or
      reconstituted instant dry milk mixed
      with 2 teaspoons vinegar

1   beaten egg, ¼ cup frozen egg substitute,
      or 2 tablespoons powdered egg substitute
      mixed with 2½ tablespoons water

½   cup boiling water or ¼ cup water and ¼
      cup orange juice

QUICK CHOCOLATE CAKE — *Continued*

Mix together flour, sugar, soda, salt, cocoa, and cinnamon in 1-quart bowl.

Mix together oil, buttermilk, and egg; then add to dry ingredients, stirring until well blended. Add boiling water and mix very well. Pour into greased 1½-quart oblong baking pan.

Bake in oven preheated to 350°F. for 30 to 35 minutes, or until center springs back when pressed with finger. Frost with Easy Chocolate Frosting (p. 000).

Makes six 2½ x 3-inch pieces.

Notes:

Easy Chocolate Frosting

   1 tablespoon cornstarch

   1 tablespoon cocoa or carob powder

   ½ cup milk or skim, 2% fat or reconstituted
       instant dry milk

   ¼ cup margarine or butter

   ¼ teaspoon imitation butter flavoring,
       if margarine is used (optional)

   ½ cup sugar or granulated sugar replacement

   ⅛ teaspoon salt or salt substitute

   ¼ teaspoon vanilla extract

       Powdered sugar (optional)

Mix cornstarch with cocoa in 2-cup saucepan. Add
milk, margarine, imitation butter flavoring, sugar, and
salt; then cook over medium-low heat until thickened
and consistency of very thick pudding. Add vanilla
extract and mix well. If a firmer frosting is desired,
add powdered sugar until frosting is consistency for
spreading.

Frosts one 5 x 9-inch cake.

Lemonade or Limeade Cake

The velvety texture of cheesecake is delightful teamed with the tanginess of lemons or limes.

9-ounce package white cake mix

½ cup plus 2 tablespoons sour cream or sour cream substitute

2 tablespoons frozen lemonade or limeade concentrate, thawed

2 eggs, ½ cup frozen egg substitute, or 2-egg size envelope powdered egg substitute mixed with ⅓ cup water

Mix together cake mix, sour cream, lemonade, and eggs in 1-quart mixing bowl until smooth and free of lumps.

Pour into well-greased 4-cup mold, bundt pan, or 1½-quart baking dish.

Bake in oven preheated to 350°F. for about 40 minutes, or until center springs back when pressed with finger. Cool and frost with Sour Cream Topping.

About 5 servings.

Continued on following page

LEMONADE OR LIMEADE CAKE
— *Continued*

SOUR CREAM TOPPING

½ cup sour cream or sour cream substitute

 3 tablespoons sugar or granulated sugar
   replacement

¼ teaspoon vanilla extract

Combine all ingredients in small bowl or cup. Spread over top of cake.

Notes:

Orange or Lemon Butter-Cream Frosting

A wonderful choice for frosting Feather-Light White Cake (p. 317).

3 tablespoons very soft butter or margarine

⅛ teaspoon salt or salt substitute

1½ cups powdered sugar

1 to 2 tablespoons orange or lemon juice

1 teaspoon grated orange peel or lemon peel

Cream together butter, salt, and powdered sugar, adding orange or lemon juice in the amount needed to make frosting consistency for spreading. Add orange or lemon peel.

Orange-Date Holiday Cake

½ cup sugar or granulated sugar replacement

¼ cup margarine or shortening

1 egg, ¼ cup frozen egg substitute, or 2 tablespoons powdered egg substitute mixed with 2½ tablespoons water

¾ cup unsifted flour

¼ teaspoon salt or salt substitute

½ teaspoon baking powder or low-sodium baking powder

½ teaspoon baking soda or low-sodium baking soda

⅓ cup buttermilk, sour cream, or sour cream substitute

¼ teaspoon imitation butter flavoring (optional)

1½ teaspoons grated orange rind

½ cup cut-up dates

¼ cup chopped nuts

2 tablespoons orange liqueur (optional)

ORANGE-DATE HOLIDAY CAKE
— *Continued*

Cream sugar with margarine in 1-quart mixing bowl; add egg and beat well.

Mix flour with salt, baking powder, and soda. Add to creamed mixture alternately with milk. Fold in grated orange rind, dates, nuts, and orange liqueur. Pour into 7½ x 3½ x 2¼-inch greased loaf pan.

Bake in oven preheated to 350°F. for 35 to 50 min. **Makes 8 slices.**

Notes:

Peach Upside Down Cake

Many fruits come in small-size cans, and there is a good selection of calorie-reduced fruits for those on special diets.

2 tablespoons margarine or butter

2 tablespoons brown sugar or brown
sugar replacement

⅛ teaspoon ground cinnamon

8¾-ounce can sliced peaches or calorie-
reduced peaches, drained

⅓ cup sugar or granulated sugar replacement

½ cup unsifted flour

1 teaspoon baking powder or low-sodium
substitute

½ teaspoon salt or salt substitute

1 well-beaten egg, ¼ cup frozen egg
substitute, or 2 tablespoons powdered
egg substitute mixed with 2½
tablespoons water

1 tablespoon plus 1 teaspoon cooking oil

PEACH UPSIDE DOWN CAKE
— *Continued*

⅓ cup buttermilk or milk, skim, 2% fat or reconstituted instant dry milk mixed with 2 teaspoons vinegar

½ teaspoon vanilla extract

Ice cream, ice milk, cream, polyunsaturated non-dairy cream, or whipped low-calorie dessert topping

Melt margarine with brown sugar and cinnamon in bottom of 7-inch pie plate, baking dish, or skillet. Remove from oven and arrange peaches in brown sugar syrup in desired design.

Mix together granulated sugar, flour, baking powder, and salt in 1-quart bowl.

Beat egg in measuring cup; then add oil, buttermilk, and vanilla extract. Add to dry ingredients, stirring until well blended. Pour batter over peaches and syrup, but don't be concerned if syrup seeps up around batter.

Bake in oven preheated to 375°F. for about 25 minutes, or until center springs back when pressed with finger. Serve with ice cream, cream, or whipped topping.

Makes four 3 x 3-inch pieces.

Rhubarb Cake

¼ cup shortening or margarine

¾ cup firmly packed brown sugar or brown sugar replacement

1 egg, ¼ cup frozen egg substitute, or 2 tablespoons powdered egg substitute mixed with 2½ tablespoons water

½ cup buttermilk or ½ cup milk or skim, 2% fat or reconstituted instant dry milk mixed with 2 teaspoons vinegar

½ teaspoon baking soda or low-sodium substitute

½ teaspoon vanilla extract

¼ teaspoon salt or salt substitute

1 cup unsifted flour

1 cup finely chopped rhubarb

⅓ cup sugar or granulated sugar replacement

¾ teaspoon ground cinnamon

1⅜-ounce package sliced almonds (optional)

RHUBARB CAKE — *Continued*

Cream shortening with brown sugar in 1-quart bowl; then add egg and beat very well.

Mix buttermilk with soda and vanilla extract.

Mix salt and flour; then add alternately with buttermilk to creamed mixture. Fold in rhubarb and pour into greased 1½-quart baking dish.

Mix together sugar and cinnamon in small bowl or cup; then sprinkle over batter. Evenly distribute slivered almonds over top.

Bake in oven preheated to 375°F. for 35 to 45 minutes, or until center springs back when pressed with finger.

Makes six 2½ x 3-inch pieces.

Notes:

Spice Cake

¼ cup butter or margarine

½ cup sugar or granulated sugar replacement

1 beaten egg, ¼ cup frozen egg substitute,
    or 2 tablespoons powdered egg
    substitute mixed with 2½ tablespoons
    water

1 tablespoon molasses or honey

½ cup buttermilk or milk, skim, 2% fat or
    reconstituted instant dry milk mixed
    with 2 teaspoons vinegar

1 cup unsifted flour

½ teaspoon soda or low-sodium substitute

¼ teaspoon salt or salt substitute

¼ teaspoon ground nutmeg

¼ teaspoon ground cloves

½ teaspoon cinnamon

SPICE CAKE — *Continued*

Cream butter with sugar in 1-quart mixing bowl; then add beaten egg, molasses, and buttermilk, blending thoroughly.

Mix together flour, soda, salt, nutmeg, cloves, and cinnamon in small bowl or cup; then gradually add to creamed mixture, blending until smooth. Pour into greased 1½-quart baking dish.

Bake in oven preheated to 375°F. for 35 minutes, or until center springs back when pressed with finger. Frost with Broiled Frosting (p. 316).

Makes six 2½ x 3-inch pieces.

Notes:

Broiled Frosting

2 tablespoons softened butter or margarine

2 tablespoons coffee cream, polyunsaturated
   non-dairy cream, or evaporated milk

¼ cup firmly packed brown sugar or brown
   sugar replacement

½ cup shredded coconut

Combine all ingredients in small bowl and mix well.
Spread over hot cake and run under broiler 4 inches
from element or flame for a few minutes or until bubbling and golden brown.

Frosts one 5 x 9-inch cake.

Notes:

Feather-Light White Cake

Gone are the days of sifting five times and the hold-your-breath, hope-it-works fever that formerly accompanied the baking of "delicate" cakes.

1¼ cups unsifted flour

2 teaspoons baking powder or low-sodium substitute

⅓ cup very soft butter, margarine or shortening

¾ cup sugar or granulated sugar replacement

1 teaspoon vanilla extract or ½ teaspoon vanilla extract and ½ teaspoon almond extract

¼ teaspoon imitation butter flavoring, if using margarine or shortening

½ cup water

3 egg whites

Continued on following page

FEATHER-LIGHT WHITE CAKE
— *Continued*

Measure flour in measuring cup; then add baking powder and mix thoroughly. Set aside.

Cream butter with sugar, vanilla extract, and butter flavoring. Add flour to creamed mixture alternately with water, beginning and ending with flour.

Beat egg whites in 2-cup bowl until stiff. Gently fold into batter. Pour into greased 1½-quart baking dish.

Bake in oven preheated to 350°F. for about 35 minutes, or until center springs back when pressed with finger. Cool and frost with Orange or Lemon Butter-Cream Frosting (p. 307) or other frosting of choice.

Makes six 2½ x 3-inch pieces.

Notes:

Cookies

Jelly or Jam Bars

½ cup soft margarine or butter

½ cup sugar or granulated sugar
    replacement

1 beaten egg, ¼ cup frozen egg substitute,
    or 2 tablespoons powdered egg
    substitute mixed with 2½ tablespoons
    water

⅓ cup milk

¼ teaspoon vanilla extract

¼ teaspoon almond extract

¼ teaspoon imitation butter flavoring,
    if using margarine (optional)

1⅓ cups unsifted flour

½ teaspoon baking powder or low-sodium
    substitute

¼ teaspoon ground cloves (optional)

½ cup strawberry, raspberry, cherry, or
    other jelly of choice or strawberry,
    raspberry, apricot, or other jam of
    choice

Continued on following page

JELLY OR JAM BARS — *Continued*

Cream margarine with sugar in 1-quart bowl; then add egg, milk, vanilla extract, almond extract, and butter flavoring. Beat vigorously until well blended.

Mix together flour, baking powder, and cloves; then add gradually to creamed mixture. Spread batter into greased 7-inch baking dish and spread jelly or jam evenly over top.

Bake in oven preheated to 350°F. for 30 to 40 minutes, or until lightly browned and done in center.

Makes twelve 1½ x 2-inch bars.

Notes:

•Peanut Butter Bars

⅓ cup peanut butter or diet-pack peanut butter

⅓ cup margarine or butter

½ teaspoon vanilla extract

¾ cup firmly packed brown sugar or brown sugar replacement

¼ teaspoon salt or salt substitute

1 egg, ¼ cup frozen egg substitute, or 2 tablespoons powdered egg substitute mixed with 2½ tablespoons water

⅔ cup unsifted flour

¼ cup finely chopped peanuts, dates, or chocolate bits (optional)

Cream peanut butter with margarine in 1-quart bowl; then add vanilla extract, brown sugar, and salt, mixing until well blended.

Slightly beat egg and add to creamed mixture; then gradually add flour and mix until smooth and creamy. Fold in chopped nuts. Spread into greased 7-inch square pan.

Bake in oven preheated to 350°F. for about 30 minutes. May be frosted with Broiled Frosting (p. 000) while still hot.

Makes about ten 1½ x 2-inch bars.

Saucepan Brownies

Gout sufferers will welcome carob powder as a chocolate substitute that will allow them chocolate flavoring without the unwanted side effects.

⅓   cup shortening or margarine

⅓   cup cocoa or carob powder

1   cup sugar or granulated sugar replacement

¼   cup milk or skim, 2% fat or reconstituted
      instant dry milk

⅓   cup unsifted flour

¼   teaspoon baking powder or low-sodium
      substitute

½   teaspoon salt or salt substitute

2   well-beaten eggs, ½ cup frozen egg
      substitute, or 2-egg size envelope
      powdered egg substitute mixed with ⅓
      cup water

½   teaspoon vanilla extract or ¼ teaspoon
      vanilla extract and few drops peppermint

½   cup finely chopped nuts or toasted soy nuts

SAUCEPAN BROWNIES — *Continued*

Melt shortening and cocoa together in 3-cup saucepan; then add sugar and milk and bring to boil. Remove from heat.

Mix flour with baking powder and salt in measuring cup; then add to hot mixture and stir until smooth.

Add eggs and vanilla extract, beating vigorously until all ingredients are blended; then fold in nuts. Pour into well-greased 8-inch square baking dish.

Bake in oven preheated to 350°F. for 25 to 30 minutes. Frost with Chocolate Frosting (p. 326).

Makes 9 to 10 bars.

Notes:

Chocolate Frosting

¼ cup cocoa or carob powder

 2 tablespoons margarine or butter

¼ teaspoon salt or salt substitute

½ teaspoon vanilla extract

1½ cups powdered sugar

 3 tablespoons milk or skim, 2% fat or
     reconstituted instant dry milk or
     coffee liqueur

Combine all ingredients in 2-cup bowl, blending until
smooth.

Notes:

Chocolate Bit Cookies

½ cup shortening or margarine

⅓ cup sugar or granulated sugar replacement

⅓ cup firmly packed brown sugar or brown
    sugar replacement

1 beaten egg, ¼ cup frozen egg substitute,
    or 2 tablespoons powdered egg
    substitute mixed with 2½ tablespoons
    water

¼ teaspoon vanilla extract

2 teaspoons water

1 cup plus 2 tablespoons unsifted flour

½ teaspoon baking soda or low-sodium
    substitute

¼ teaspoon salt or salt substitute

¾ cup chocolate bits or mini-carob bits

½ cup finely chopped nuts or toasted soy nuts
    (optional)

Continued on following page

CHOCOLATE BIT COOKIES — *Continued*

Cream shortening with sugar, brown sugar, egg, vanilla extract, and water in 1-quart bowl.

Mix together flour, soda, and salt; then gradually add to creamed mixture. Fold in chocolate bits and nuts. Drop by teaspoonfuls two inches apart onto ungreased cookie sheet.

Bake in oven preheated to 350°F. for about 10 to 12 minutes.

Makes 2½ to 3 dozen cookies.

ALTERNATE I: For High-Protein Cereal Cookies: Add 1 cup high protein cereal flakes with chocolate bits, or chocolate bits may be omitted.

ALTERNATE II: For Applesauce-Raisin Cookies: Add 1 cup applesauce, 1 teaspoon ground cinnamon, ½ teaspoon ground nutmeg, 2 teaspoons baking powder, 2 cups quick rolled oats and increase flour to 2 cups. Substitute raisins for chocolate bits.

⌀Nutritious Cookies

If you make these extra-large, one is a very energizing component of a satisfying, but unusual breakfast.

⅓ cup cooking oil

⅔ cup honey or molasses

1 egg, ¼ cup frozen egg substitute, or 2 tablespoons powdered egg substitute mixed with 2½ tablespoons water

1 teaspoon vanilla extract

½ cup raisins or ¼ cup raisins and ¼ cup toasted soy nuts

¾ cup wheat germ

1 cup rolled oats

⅓ cup whole wheat, soy, or rice polish flour

½ teaspoon salt or salt substitute

¼ cup instant dry milk

Combine oil, honey, egg, and vanilla extract in 1-quart mixing bowl.

Mix together raisins, wheat germ, rolled oats, flour, salt, and instant dry milk in 2-cup bowl. Gradually add to oil and honey mixture and mix until well blended.

Line cookie sheet with aluminum foil or generously greased brown paper. Drop or push cookie dough from teaspoon onto greased surface.

Bake in oven preheated to 350°F. for 10 minutes.

Makes about 2 dozen cookies, depending on size.

Soft Oatmeal Cookies

1 cup unsifted flour

¾ cup sugar or granulated sugar replacement

¼ teaspoon salt or salt substitute

¼ teaspoon baking soda or low-sodium substitute

½ teaspoon ground cinnamon

¼ teaspoon ground cloves

½ cup shortening or margarine

1 egg, ¼ cup frozen egg substitute, or 2 tablespoons powdered egg substitute mixed with 2½ tablespoons water

⅓ cup buttermilk or milk or skim, 2% fat or reconstituted instant dry milk mixed with 2 teaspoons vinegar

¾ cup quick-cooking rolled oats

½ cup raisins

½ cup chopped nuts or toasted soy nuts (optional)

SOFT OATMEAL COOKIES — *Continued*

Mix together flour, sugar, salt, soda, cinnamon, and cloves in 1-quart mixing bowl. Rub in shortening with spoon; then add egg and buttermilk, beating vigorously. Stir in rolled oats, raisins, and nuts; then blend very well and refrigerate for few hours.

Drop by teaspoonfuls about 2 inches apart on greased baking sheet.

Bake in oven preheated to 350°F. for 10 to 12 min.

Makes about 3 dozen cookies.

Notes:

Small-Batch Cookies

6 tablespoons soft margarine or butter

⅓ cup unsifted flour

¼ cup cornstarch

6 tablespoons sugar or granulated sugar replacement

¼ teaspoon vanilla or lemon extract or ¼ teaspoon vanilla and ¼ teaspoon almond extracts

¼ cup very finely chopped nuts (optional)

Place margarine in 3-cup bowl.

Mix together flour, cornstarch, and sugar; then gradually add to margarine, mixing until smooth and well blended. Add vanilla extract; then fold in nuts.

Form dough into 1-inch balls and place on ungreased cookie sheet 1½ inches apart; then flatten with fork.

Bake in oven preheated to 325°F. for 15 to 20 minutes. Remove from cookie sheet immediately.

Makes about 1½ dozen cookies.

Sugar Cookies

These do not require rolling-out the dough and cutting into shapes.

½ cup sugar or granulated sugar replacement

½ cup butter or margarine

1 egg, separated

1 cup unsifted flour

½ teaspoon ground cinnamon

½ teaspoon vanilla extract

Cream sugar with butter in 1-quart bowl; then add egg yolk and beat vigorously.

Mix flour and cinnamon; then add gradually to creamed mixture. Add vanilla extract.

Thinly spread out dough on cookie sheet.

Beat egg white slightly and coat surface of dough. Sprinkle with additional sugar, if desired.

Bake in oven preheated to 300°F. for 15 to 20 minutes. Cut immediately, but let cool in pan.

Makes about 1 dozen cookies.

PIES

All-In-One Apple Pie

Pressured for time? This is your answer. The cake-like pastry and fruit are quickly tossed together in a one-bowl, three-step procedure that only takes a few minutes.

1 egg, ¼ cup frozen egg substitute, or 2
    tablespoons powdered egg substitute
    mixed with 2½ tablespoons water

¼ teaspoon vanilla extract

⅔ cup sugar or granulated sugar replacement

2 tablespoons flour

1 teaspoon baking powder or low-sodium
    substitute

¼ teaspoon salt or salt substitute

½ cup chopped apple

2 teaspoons lemon juice

½ cup chopped nuts (optional)

    Ice cream, ice milk, dietetic ice cream,
    whipped cream, whipped low-calorie
    dessert topping, cream or
    polyunsaturated non-dairy cream

Continued on following page

ALL-IN-ONE APPLE PIE — *Continued*

Beat egg, vanilla extract, and sugar together very vigorously in 1-quart bowl.

Mix together flour, baking powder, and salt in small
bowl or cup; then gradually add to egg mixture.

Mix apples with lemon juice and fold into batter;
then add nuts. Pour into greased 7-inch baking dish
or pie plate.

Bake in oven preheated to 350°F. for about 30 minutes. Serve with ice cream, whipped cream, or cream.

Makes about 4 servings.

Notes:

New Method Apple Pie

If you choose not to get out your rolling pin, you will like this quick way to a pleasing, delicately flavored pie.

Pastry for 7-inch, 1-crust pie, or Oil Pastry
   recipe (p. 358), or 1 pie crust stick
   (one-half 11-ounce package)

2 large apples or 1½ cups canned apple
   slices

1 tablespoon lemon juice (about ½ lemon)

2 tablespoons honey

3 whole cloves

¼ teaspoon ground cinnamon

2 teaspoons butter

Sugar or granulated sugar replacement

NEW METHOD APPLE PIE — *Continued*

Set aside 2 tablespoons pastry; then pat and press with fingers remaining pastry into 7-inch pie plate, fluting the edge.

Peel, core, then slice apples into 3-cup saucepan with cover. Add lemon juice, honey, cloves, and cinnamon. Cook over medium-low heat until tender, adding no water. If using canned apples, follow same procedure, but reduce cooking time. Remove from heat and remove whole cloves.

Pour apple mixture into pie shell; then sprinkle remaining pastry over the top of apples by gently rubbing between fingers. Sprinkle with sugar and additional cinnamon, if desired.

Bake in oven preheated to 400°F. for about 40 min. **Makes 4 servings.**

Notes:

Cherry Pie

Many times individual desserts serve the most situations and occasions. If frozen, they are quickly thawed and made table-ready. Consider making tarts, or discover the packaged crumb and pastry tart shells at the market. Frozen, then baked, patty shells serve well, too.

1½ cups frozen or canned cherries

⅓ cup cherry juice or cherry juice and water to make ⅓ cup

2 teaspoons cornstarch

3 tablespoons sugar or granulated sugar replacement

3 drops almond extract

2 teaspoons butter or margarine

⅛ teaspoon salt or salt substitute

1 teaspoon lemon juice

Baked 7-inch pastry shell or 4 tart or patty shells

Ice cream, ice milk, dietetic ice cream, whipped cream or low-calorie dessert topping or frozen non-dairy dessert topping

Continued on following page

CHERRY PIE — *Continued*

If using frozen cherries, place cherries in 3-cup saucepan with cover and simmer without additional water over low heat for about 15 to 20 minutes, or until completely thawed, but just cooked.

If using canned cherries, drain and remeasure correct amount of juice.

Mix cherry juice with cornstarch, sugar, almond extract, butter, salt, and lemon juice. Blend with cherries and cook over medium-low heat, stirring frequently, until thickened. Pour into baked pie shell or tart shells. Serve with ice cream or whipped cream.
4 servings.

ALTERNATE I: For Blueberry Pie: Substitute blueberries for cherries and ⅛ teaspoon ground cinnamon and ⅛ teaspoon ground nutmeg for almond extract.

ALTERNATE II: For Blackberry or Raspberry Pie: Substitute blackberries or raspberries for cherries and ⅛ teaspoon ground cinnamon and ⅛ teaspoon ground cloves for almond extract.

ALTERNATE III: For Berry- or Cherry-Cream Cheese Pie: Soften 3-ounce package cream cheese and mix with 1 tablespoon milk or cream. Spread in bottom of baked pie shell or tart shells, then proceed as directed for Cherry, Blueberry, Blackberry, or Raspberry Pie.

Vanilla Cream Pie

And vanilla is only the beginning with this basic recipe.
From its good beginning come many-flavored endings.

  5 tablespoons packaged vanilla pudding
       and pie filling, 2 tablespoons low-calorie
       pudding and pie filling mix, or 2½
       tablespoons Easy Pudding Mix (p. 258)

1¼ cups milk or skim, 2% fat or reconstituted
       instant dry milk

  1 teaspoon butter or margarine

  ¼ teaspoon imitation butter flavoring,
       if using margarine (optional)

  ¼ cup low-calorie dessert topping mix

       Baked 7-inch pastry or crumb shell or
       4 tart or patty shells

Mix pudding and pie filling with 1 cup milk in 2-cup saucepan; then cook over medium-low heat until very thick. Remove from heat and add butter or imitation butter flavoring. Cover with plastic wrap or waxed paper and refrigerate until cool.

Whip dessert topping mix with remaining ¼ cup milk. Fold into cooled pudding; then pour into baked

Continued on following page

VANILLA CREAM PIE — *Continued*

pastry shell or individual shells. May be served with additional whipped topping and shaved chocolate, if desired.

3 to 4 servings.

ALTERNATE I: For Rum Cream Pie: Substitute 2 tablespoons rum for vanilla extract.

ALTERNATE II: For Chocolate Rum Pie: Use chocolate flavored pudding and pie filling mix and substitute 2 tablespoons rum for vanilla extract.

ALTERNATE III: For Banana Cream Pie: Slice 1 large banana into cooled pastry shell; then pour vanilla cream pie filling over bananas.

ALTERNATE IV: For Butterscotch Cream Pie: Substitute butterscotch-flavored pudding and pie filling and increase butter to 1 tablespoon.

ALTERNATE V: For Coconut Cream Pie: Add ½ cup shredded or flaked coconut to vanilla cream pie filling; then sprinkle a little additional coconut over top.

ALTERNATE VI: For Chocolate Peppermint Pie: Use chocolate-flavored pudding and pie filling mix and add 3 drops peppermint extract.

ALTERNATE VII: For Vanilla Cream Pie with Currant Jelly Glaze: Melt ¼ cup currant jelly with 2 teaspoons orange liqueur, if desired, and pour over cooled cream filling.

No-Egg Lemon Pie

This meets the requirements of most diets.

     1 cup sugar or granulated sugar
          replacement

   ¼ cup cornstarch

1 ½ cups water

     3 drops yellow food coloring

     3 tablespoons margarine or butter

   ¼ cup lemon juice

1 ½ teaspoons grated lemon rind

          Baked 7-inch pastry or crumb shell or
            4 tart or patty shells

          Whipped low-calorie dessert topping
            or frozen dessert topping

Combine sugar, cornstarch, water, and food coloring
in 2-cup saucepan. Cook over medium-low heat, stirring continually until thickened.

   Remove from heat and add margarine, lemon juice,
and lemon rind, stirring until margarine is melted.
Pour into baked pastry shell or individual shells. Top
with whipped topping.

3 to 4 servings.

Lime Pie

1 beaten egg, ¼ cup frozen egg substitute, or 2 tablespoons powdered egg substitute mixed with 2½ tablespoons water

5⅓-ounce can evaporated milk or ⅔ cup 99% fat-free skimmed milk

3 tablespoons sugar or granulated sugar replacement

3 tablespoons lime juice (about 1 lime)

½ teaspoon grated lime rind

Baked 7-inch crumb or pastry shell

Whipped cream or low-calorie dessert topping or frozen non-dairy whipped topping

Beat egg vigorously in 2-cup bowl. Gradually add milk; then sugar. Add lime juice and pour into baked crumb or pastry shell.

Bake in oven preheated to 300°F. for 35 to 40 minutes. Serve with whipped cream or whipped topping.

3 to 4 servings.

ALTERNATE: For Lemon Pie: Substitute lemon juice for lime juice.

Fresh Peach Pie

Pastry for 7-inch 2-crust pie or 1 recipe
Pastry for 2-Crust Pie (p. 000)

1 tablespoon lemon juice

¼ teaspoon almond extract

1 tablespoon cognac or brandy (optional)

2½ cups sliced fresh peaches

⅓ cup sugar or granulated sugar replacement

1 tablespoon quick-cooking tapioca

⅛ teaspoon ground nutmeg

¼ teaspoon salt or salt substitute

1 tablespoon butter or margarine

Roll out half the pastry and line 7-inch pie plate.

Mix together lemon juice, almond extract, and cognac in bottom of 1-quart bowl; then add peaches and stir gently to blend.

Mix together sugar, tapioca, nutmeg, and salt in small bowl or cup. Pour over fruit and gently stir until fruit is well-coated with sugar mixture. Spread fruit evenly in pastry-lined pie plate and dot with butter.

Roll out remaining pastry and place over peaches. Trim and flute edge. Sprinkle with additional sugar or brush with slightly beaten egg white, if desired.

3 to 4 servings.

Pumpkin Chiffon Pie

If you have leftover pumpkin, you'll enjoy Pumpkin Bread (p. 277).

1½ teaspoons unflavored gelatin

⅓ cup sugar or granulated sugar replacement

⅛ teaspoon ground ginger

¼ teaspoon ground nutmeg

¼ teaspoon ground cinnamon

¼ teaspoon salt or salt substitute

½ cup pumpkin

¾ cup milk or skim, 2% fat or reconstituted instant dry milk

¼ cup low-calorie dessert topping mix

1 tablespoon rum (optional)

6- or 7-inch baked pie shell (p. 357), or Crumb Crust (p. 355), or 1 pie crust stick (one-half 11-ounce package)

PUMPKIN CHIFFON PIE — *Continued*

Mix together gelatin, sugar, ginger, nutmeg, cinnamon, and salt in 3-cup saucepan.

Mix pumpkin with ½ cup milk and egg; add to gelatin.

Cook over low heat until thickened; cool.

Beat whipped topping mix with remaining ¼ cup milk until consistency of whipped cream; add rum. Fold whipped topping into pumpkin mixture and pour into pie shell.

2 to 3 servings.

Notes:

More-Than-Rhubarb Pie

Pastry for 7-inch 1-crust pie or 1 recipe
   Oil Pastry (p. 358), or Pastry for 7-inch
   Pie (p. 357)

1 cup sugar or granulated sugar replacement

3 tablespoons flour

⅛ teaspoon ground nutmeg

¼ teaspoon ground cinnamon

¼ teaspoon salt or salt substitute

1 beaten egg, ¼ cup frozen egg substitute,
   or 2 tablespoons powdered egg
   substitute mixed with 2½ tablespoons
   water

1½ to 2 cups finely diced rhubarb

Roll out pastry and line 7-inch pie plate.

Mix sugar with flour, nutmeg, cinnamon, and salt in 1-quart bowl. Add egg and beat until well blended; then add rhubarb. Spread fruit evenly in pastry-lined pie plate.

Bake in oven preheated to 350°F. for about 1¼ hours, or until filling is thickened in center.

3 to 4 servings.

ALTERNATE: For Strawberry-Rhubarb Pie: Use 1 cup cut-up strawberries and 1 cup cut-up rhubarb.

Fresh Strawberry Pie

2 cups fresh strawberries, washed

½ cup sugar or granulated sugar replacement

2 teaspoons lemon juice

1½ tablespoons cornstarch

2 tablespoons water

Baked 7-inch pastry shell or 4 tart or patty shells

Whipped cream or low-calorie dessert topping or frozen non-dairy dessert topping

Set aside 1 cup berries.

Mash remaining cup berries with sugar and combine with lemon juice, cornstarch, and water in 2-cup saucepan. Bring to boil and cook until thickened, and sauce is clear, stirring continually.

Cut in half or leave whole, depending on size, the uncooked berries and arrange in bottom of baked pastry shell or individual shells; then pour cooked berries over top. Top with whipped cream or topping.

Makes 4 servings.

Pastry

Cereal Crumb Crust

1½ cups corn, rice, wheat, or high-protein
      cereal flakes

¼ cup sugar or granulated sugar replacement

½ teaspoon ground cinnamon

2 tablespoons very soft butter or margarine

Crush cereal flakes in plastic bag by pressing between fingers or with rolling pin on bread board.

Mix together cereal flakes, sugar, cinnamon, and butter in bottom of 7-inch pie plate with fork.

Gently press crumbs evenly over bottom and sides up to rim of pie plate.

Bake in oven preheated to 375°F. for about 8 minutes. Cool before filling.

Makes one 7-inch crumb shell.

Notes:

Crumb Crust

⅔ cup vanilla wafer crumbs
(about 15 wafers)

1 tablespoon sugar or granulated sugar
replacement

1½ tablespoons very soft butter or margarine

Blend thoroughly vanilla wafer crumbs, sugar, and butter in bottom of 7-inch pie plate with fork.

Gently press crumbs evenly over bottom and sides up to rim of pie plate.

Bake in oven preheated to 375°F. for about 8 minutes. Cool before filling.

Makes one 7-inch crumb shell.

ALTERNATE I: For Chocolate Crumb Crust: Substitute chocolate wafer crumbs for vanilla wafer crumbs.

ALTERNATE II: For Banana Crumb Crust: Substitute Banana wafer crumbs for vanilla wafer crumbs.

ALTERNATE III: For Graham Cracker Crumb Crust: Substitute graham cracker crumbs for vanilla wafer crumbs and add ⅛ teaspoon ground cinnamon, if desired.

Pastry for 7-Inch 1-Crust Pie

¾ cup unsifted flour

¼ cup shortening, margarine, or lard

¼ teaspoon salt or salt substitute

1½ to 2 tablespoons cold water

Put flour in 2-cup bowl and add shortening and salt. Cut shortening into flour with 2 knives or pastry blender until mixture resembles coarse corn meal. Sprinkle a little water at a time over flour and toss lightly with a fork after each addition.

Form dough into a ball, being careful not to handle dough more than necessary.

Roll out dough on lightly floured board into 9-inch circle and fit into pie plate, or gently press dough evenly over bottom and sides up to rim of 7-inch pie plate. Flute edge.

For baked pastry shell: Preheat oven to 450°F. and bake 8 to 10 minutes.

Makes one 7-inch shell or 4 tart shells.

Oil Pastry

1 cup unsifted flour

¼ teaspoon salt or salt substitute

¼ cup cooking oil

Mix together flour and salt in 2-cup mixing bowl. Gradually add oil until flour and oil are well blended.

Gently press pie dough evenly over bottom and sides up to rim of 7-inch pie plate. Flute edge.

For baked pastry shell: Preheat oven to 450°F. and bake 8 to 10 minutes.

Makes one 7-inch shell or 4 tart shells.

Notes:

•Sugar Cookie Crust

½ cup frozen slice-and-bake sugar cookie
     dough or one-half recipe Sugar Cookies
     (p. 333)

Thaw frozen cookie dough until soft enough to shape, but do not let get too warm or soft.

Gently press sugar cookie dough evenly over bottom and sides up to rim of 7-inch pie plate. Seal dough over edge of pie plate.

Bake in oven preheated to 375°F. for 15 minutes. **Makes one 7-inch pie shell.**

Notes:

Dietetic Foods Available at Supermarkets and Drugstores

DIETETIC BEVERAGES AND LIQUID FOODS
Diet drink mix in assorted flavors
Liquid diet food in assorted flavors
Sugar-free, calorie-reduced carbonated beverages in assorted flavors

DIETETIC BREADS, COOKIES, AND CRACKERS
Salt-free bread
Dietetic bread sticks
Dietetic cheese thins
Low-sodium cookies: Apple, chocolate chip, chocolate-filled sandwich wafers, coconut, egg biscuit, fig, kichel, lemon, oatmeal, peach-apricot, prune-flavored, vanilla-filled wafers, vanilla-chocolate-filled wafers, strawberry-filled wafers, and vanilla sandwich cookies

DIETETIC CANDIES AND CHEWING GUM
Sugarless chocolate TV mix
Sugarless hard candies
Sugarless lifesaver mints in assorted flavors

361

Sugarless licorice drops
Calorie-reduced peanut butter cups
Natural carob-covered raisins
Natural carob-covered soy beans
Dietetic assorted milk chocolates
Dietetic assorted creams
Sugarless gum in assorted flavors
Sugarless bubblegum

DIETETIC DAIRY PRODUCTS AND NON-DAIRY SUBSTITUTES

Salt-free butter
Non-dairy creamer
Non-dairy instant dry creamer
Non-dairy polyunsaturated coffee cream
Non-dairy sour cream substitute
Non-dairy whipping blend cream
Non-dairy frozen whipped topping
Low-calorie dessert topping mix
Low-fat cottage cheese
Fat-reduced cream cheese
99% fat-free process cheese product
Part-skim Danish Danbo cheese
Part-skim Danish Port Salut cheese
Part-skim Danish Tilsit cheese
Part-skim Danish Tybo cheese
Low-moisture, part-skim Mozzarella cheese
Low-moisture, part-skim Scamorza cheese
Powdered cultured buttermilk
Non-dairy instant dry milk
Salt-free margarine
Low-fat yogurt
Cholesterol-free liquid egg substitute
Frozen liquid egg substitute
Powdered egg substitute

DIETETIC DESSERTS
Low-sodium, low-calorie gelatin dessert mix in
assorted flavors
Diet pudding in assorted flavors
Low-calorie pudding and pie filling mix in assorted
flavors
Dietetic sherbets, ice creams, and ice milks in
assorted flavors
Low-calorie butterscotch topping
Low-calorie chocolate topping

DIETETIC FISH AND VEGETABLES
Tuna in water without salt
Salmon in water without salt
Green beans without salt or sugar
Whole kernel corn without salt or sugar
Green peas without salt or sugar
Tomatoes without salt or sugar

DIETETIC FRUITS (IN NATURAL JUICE OR WATER-PACKED) AND FRUIT JUICES
Diet applesauce
Diet apricot halves
Diet Royal Ann cherries
Diet Kadota figs
Diet fruit cocktail
Diet fruits for salad
Diet grapefruit sections
Diet mandarin orange sections
Diet yellow cling sliced peaches
Diet yellow cling peach halves
Diet Bartlett pear halves
Diet sliced pineapple
Diet pineapple tidbits
Diet purple plums

Unsweetened apple juice
Diet apricot juice
Low-calorie cranapple juice drink
Low-calorie cranberry juice cocktail
Unsweetened grapefruit juice
Unsweetened prune juice
Unsweetened frozen apple cider concentrate
Unsweetened frozen apple juice concentrate
Unsweetened frozen grapefruit juice concentrate
Unsweetened orange juice concentrate
Unsweetened frozen pineapple juice concentrate

DIETETIC JAMS, JELLIES, AND PRESERVES

Low-calorie blackberry, strawberry, and raspberry jam
Low-calorie apple and grape jelly
Low-calorie orange marmalade
Low-calorie cherry, boysenberry, apricot, and
  pineapple preserves
Low-calorie cranberry sauce

DIETETIC NUTS AND NUT BUTTERS

Unsalted cashew butter
Low-sodium peanut butter
Unsalted peanut butter
Calorie-reduced peanut butter
Dry-roasted, salt-free peanuts
Dry-roasted, salt-free soy beans
Toasted sea-salted soy beans
Toasted soy beans

DIETETIC SALAD DRESSINGS, SAUCES, AND SYRUP

Low-calorie Blue cheese dressing
Low-calorie coleslaw dressing
Low-calorie French dressing
Low-calorie Green Goddess dressing

Low-calorie creamy Italian dressing
Low-calorie Italian dressing
Low-fat mayonnaise
Low-calorie Russian dressing
Low-calorie Thousand Island dressing
Low-sodium, low-calorie catsup
Salt-free chili sauce
Cream (white) sauce with skim milk
Diet Worcestershire sauce
Low-calorie maple syrup

DIETETIC SALT, SUGAR, AND BAKING SUBSTITUTES

Salt substitute
Seasoned salt substitute
Vegetable salt
Seasoned vegetable salt
¼-grain saccharin, calorie-free sweetener
½-grain saccharin, calorie-free sweetener
Low-calorie liquid sugar replacement
Low-calorie powdered sugar replacement
Calorie-free brown sugar replacement
Calorie-free granulated sugar replacement
Low-sodium baking powder
Low-sodium baking soda
Low-calorie pancake and waffle mix

DIETETIC SOUPS

Low-calorie instant beef-flavored broth and seasoning
Low-calorie Borscht
Low-calorie instant chicken-flavored broth and
 seasoning
Low-sodium tomato soup
Salt-free tomato bouillon
Low-sodium turkey noodle soup
Low-sodium vegetable soup

Index